Until We Meet Again

Hera Mackiernan

Published by BookLocker.com, Inc., Bradenton, Florida, U.S.A.

Printed on acid-free paper.

BookLocker.com, Inc.
2016

First Edition

Contents

INTRODUCTION 1

CHAPTER ONE - BEING A MEDIUM 3

My experiences growing up as a child and my struggle to figure out on my own what was happening. How my abilities evolved into helping others with my gift in adulthood. I also give an explanation of how mediumship works, and why some of us have trouble connecting with the world of spirit on their own.

CHAPTER TWO - SPIRIT GUIDES 15

In this chapter I explain how everyone has a guide, and how to contact your guide. How our guides help us through life, and the importance of listening to our gut instincts. I also tell my first experience seeing my guide, how she communicates with me, and how our guides are trained on the other side before becoming guides. I also share bits of insights that have been shared over the years.

CHAPTER THREE - GHOSTS 25

I will explain why only one type of ghost can exist. Why spirits of children never become ghosts. Why ghosts stay behind, my first experience with a haunting when I was a child, and my second as an adult. I also include ways to make your home more comfortable while living with a ghost.

CHAPTER FOUR - ASTRAL TRAVEL AND DREAMS 35

I explain the difference between the two. How to recognize a visit with a loved one while in the dream state. How to recognize a dream of or from the other side. And what an astral travel experience is like.

CHAPTER FIVE - REINCARNATION............................ 49

A brief history of reincarnation and the religions that embrace the belief. How your past life(s) weave themselves into your present incarnation. How to discover which points in time your soul experienced. My previous incarnations, and how I believe they have influenced my present incarnation.

CHAPTER SIX - THE ARCHANGELS AND MARY MAGDALENE 59

The roles of the Archangels throughout history. Messages from the Angels received during meditation, how you can call on them for guidance and protection. New and never before channeled information about the real relationship between Jesus and Mary Magdalene.

CHAPTER SEVEN - MESSAGES FROM HOME 73

What life is like for our loved ones living on the other side. What kinds of signs they send us, what it is like to cross over to the other side.

CHAPTER EIGHT - ANATOMY OF A READING 83

I breakdown a reading into its individual parts, from start to finish to help explain the reading process. Why and how some information gets missed by the reader.

CHAPTER NINE - HOW TO RAISE A PSYCHIC CHILD 95

My goal with this chapter is to assist parents who are not psychic themselves, handle raising a child that has the gift, without fear, and with understanding.

CHAPTER 10 - THE FUTURE OF MEDIUMSHIP....... 101

How mediums that are in the public eye today, are changing people's understanding of spirit communication, and helping people heal from loss.

Introduction

What is it like to be a psychic medium? To communicate with and feel the world of spirit every day? Sharing my gift is the most beautiful experience. To bring a message to a grieving soul. To connect two souls disconnected by time and space. What is it like to be me? For me it feels natural to communicate with spirit. It wasn't always natural to let my gift be known. Being raised in a religious household, unforgiving of who I was, who I was born to be, how God created me. I was met with harsh words and criticism when I tried to express what was happening. I was all alone and very out of place in my family. I was told I was crazy, lying, and if I was telling the truth, well I was doomed to spend an eternity in hell. Being told these things, and treated this way, simply made the wall I was building between myself and my family higher and thicker. I knew what I was experiencing was real. I had many validations that reminded me constantly. It was a long process to let go of the fear of how negative skeptical people would react when the words "I'm a psychic medium" would tumble out from my mouth. I expected to be met with a barrage of insults from most.

Now my work as a psychic medium has turned out to be one of the most amazing and fulfilling experiences of my life. I want to share my gift with as many souls as possible, just as was intended when I was born.

Along with connecting with spirit for clients, I am able to channel messages from the Archangels. The messages that I channel are for every soul here on earth to gather meaning from. I was also able to channel a message from Mary Magdalene. I believe she came to me, for the simple fact that I shunned what I was taught about her at church, I intuitively knew it was not true. Her spirit knew I was open to absolutely anything she needed or wanted to communicate. Not just to me but to the world.

Our loved ones who have crossed over, want us to know they are ok, happy, loved, at peace and are existing in the most beautiful place anyone could imagine being.

Deep in our hearts and souls we know this, but existing in this physical body, with our human minds we simply forget.

I and other mediums are your reminder, that life is a beautiful thing, and our loved ones want us to live it to the fullest, until it is our time to return home to the other side, and meet again.

Chapter One

Being A Medium

My first experiences with the spirit world began with watching spirits wander around the shadows of my bedroom. My solution was to keep my bedroom light on all night. Which was foolproof until my father walked by on his way to bed and ordered me to shut the light off. I had him outsmarted though. I simply pulled the covers over my head as if they acted like a paranormal shield that would protect me from the shadowy unknown. I used my blanket shield until I began to hear the loud house shaking snoring pouring from the back bedroom. Snoring started, blanket shield down, light back on, it was the perfect plan. Finally I close my tired eyes to get some much needed sleep and feel the edge of my bed move as if someone had just walked in my room and plopped themselves down by my feet. I open my eyes to see there is an impression on the blankets but of course no one visible there to see. I sigh and mumble under my breath if your going to disturb me the least you could do is show yourself to me. Once again I close my eyes and drift off to a not very restful dreamland. What follows is a night filled with dreams of the next day news events, celebrity deaths, plane crashes, ships sinking. All of which I experience with vivid detail.

In the morning I woke up exhausted as if I hadn't slept a wink. I wanted so much to make sense of what was going on. Finally I worked up the nerve to tell my parents what was going on. I was finally going to tell them about this amazing magical experience I had where I could see the future! In a nut shell I was left disappointed after being told it was just my imagination and to stop making things up. My I have super powers bubble was deflated and I was left scratching my head. I knew I was telling the truth why were they not believing me? I reminded my self of the validations I had experienced, over and over again. And was left frustrated with my parents. I decided I was never going to mention any of this again and keep my experiences to myself. I began to ignore and suppress my psychic abilities, it was like trying not to breathe, and yet somehow stay alive. This left me struggling with why in the world did I have this stinking ability if I have to keep it to myself? At the same time my psychic experiences were keeping my spiritual faith intact and alive while experiencing a childhood that very easily could of created an atheist.

It wasn't until I hit my teenage years I decided I was going to get to the bottom of this once and for all, and started searching the new age section of my local bookstore for answers, no google back then ha! I flipped through some books and finally bought a few. What I read was so comforting and it was a breath of fresh air to know I really wasn't alone in the world. I still wasn't comfortable talking about any of this with my family or friends. After my parents divorce I did feel slightly more comfortable mentioning my dreams to my mother, she was slightly more open minded then my father, but I got a mixed reaction from her. One example of this confusing response from her was when one of my older brothers had come over for a visit. He was attending college a few towns over. The night before he visited I had experienced a vivid dream where I was riding in the passenger side of my mother's car and she was driving. While we were driving around in the dark, we saw two teenage girls walking on the side of the road. As we approached them in the car, the car suddenly swerved off the road and started speeding toward the girls. The car hit one of the young girls, she smacked the windshield, with a look of horror on her face as she bounced off the car and landed on the side of the road. When it was time to drive my brother back to college, I insisted on going for the ride with them. My intuition was screaming at the top of its lungs that the dream was about that night! I was way to nervous and anxious to stay home by myself. I was convinced if I went with them I could warn her of impending danger. The trip back to my brother's college went off without a hitch. We dropped him off, said our goodbyes and I switched my seat, and buckled myself safely into the passenger side of my mother's tiny blue Toyota Celica. Off we went headed down a poorly lit Massachusetts small town road, which could be kind of creepy at that time of night. I was still convinced my mother was about to commit vehicular homicide, and she was thoroughly annoyed with my begging and pleading with her to turn around and take another route home. My anxiety was through the roof as my horrible dream was unfolding before my eyes. She told me to stop panicking nothing was going to happen. A few moments later we turned down yet another poorly lit road, and ended up behind a huge gray pick up truck. A moment or so later we saw the teenage girls from my dream walking on the side of the road. I immediately pointed them out to her and said please be careful as we approached. My mother tried to hide her fear but it was written all over her face. Suddenly out of nowhere the gray truck in front of us swerved and started speeding right toward the girls. He swerved right back onto the road seconds before he was about to hit them, as if he was playing chicken with them. Thankfully no one was hurt and we continued on our way back home. My mother was truly shocked and amazed by what happened. And finally acknowledged that the only way I could of known what was going to happen that night was that I was psychic. The following day I overheard her talking about it on the phone with a friend. Then it was never mentioned again. It was like it never happened. Looking back, she likely had no idea what to make of the incident, what meaning it might have had or was afraid of how others would perceive her for acknowledging what had happened. I have no idea what she was thinking. For me it was quite obviously a warning for her to be careful at that particular moment in time. But her reaction confused and angered me. I had proven myself psychically finally after not being believed for so long and pretty much got a slap in the face for it. So once again I made my mind up I was never going to mention any of this again. I put my books away and was back to trying not to breathe again.

I continued to have prophetic dreams not only about others but about important events in my own life as well. I had a vision of meeting my first husband about a week before we met. The vision was so vivid I knew it was him as soon as I saw him, and when he told me the name of the street he lived on in Plymouth, this was even more validation that it was him I had the vision about. This also happened with my second husband as well. When we were being introduced, as soon as I finished the sentence, hi nice to meet you, something whispered in my ear, this is the man you are going to marry and spend the rest of your life with. Well as soon as that thought left my bubble, I thought to myself wow I must really be losing it. I was instantly attracted to him, but the thought of us getting together at that time seemed impossible and crazy. I was already unhappily married with no plans at that time of leaving even though I was not happy in the marriage. The feeling I had seemed so right even though it made no sense what so ever at the time. In the days and weeks that followed, just about every night I experienced vivid dreams of my self and this man I just met, together as a happy couple. It seemed so real when I woke up in the morning I was so confused I really thought I was losing it. Then to top it off, one afternoon when I was napping before the school bus dropped off my oldest two sons, I experienced a vision of this cute little baby boy smiling at me wearing nothing but a diaper. Something said to me, this is your future son that you are going to have with the man you just met. When I woke up confusion set in once again. The vision felt so right and I knew in my heart that baby boy was mine. I knew without a doubt that this was going to happen even though it seemed so impossible at that time in our lives. Eventually we did get together, and we now have two amazing girls and that same cute little baby boy, who gave me a major deja-vu moment when he was just six months old, smiling at me wearing nothing but a diaper. Though these visions were hard for me to decipher a the moment I had them, they have given me personally the evidence I needed that our bodies do in fact contain a soul.

From my experiences and some of what I have read I have come up with what I feel is a proper definition and explanation of what psychic abilities are, and how they function. The terms I am using describing the six parts of what I call the sixth sense, I learned during my mediumship certification course. I feel psychic abilities function as a sixth sense. Most of us are born with some sort of psychic awareness, with varying degrees of effectiveness. Although there are some people who are born with a sixth sense that does not work, just as some of us are born blind or deaf. I believe this explains why not everyone believes in what my self and other mediums do. They simply have no concept, its comparable to trying to describe the color red to someone who has never seen color. I also feel telling everyone that they can connect with spirit is misleading for the psychically deaf. It seems so un fair to the individual who really wants to connect with a loved one who has crossed over and simply can't through no fault of their own. They may come to the conclusion they have done something wrong concerning their loved one, the loved one doesn't want to communicate with them, or the loved one didn't cross over and is not happy or at peace on the other side.

That being said, those who are born with some psychic ability can strengthen their senses. In this way I like to compare the sixth sense with artistic and musical talents. Most of us have the capacity to pick up a pencil and draw a picture of some sort, and possibly improve our drawing technique with the aid of art lessons. There are some highly talented individuals who can pick up a pencil and create an awe inspiring work of art with little or no training. Again, another way of looking at the sixth sense is to compare it with the other five senses we all know so well. Many of us are born into the world with 20/20 vision. Some will be born needing some type of corrective lens to see clearly. Unfortunately some of us are born into this life blind. So it is with psychic abilities, most of us can be taught to some degree, to use our sixth sense effectively, and experience a glimpse into the world of spirit. I'm the artist who never needed an art lesson. Psychic events are something that came as naturally to me as breathing.

Psychics will utilize the other five senses in conjunction with the sixth sense when connecting with the world of spirit. Along with that the sixth sense is a combination of six different types of psychic awareness. They are claircognance, clairvoyant awareness, clairentient, clairaudience, clairgustance, and finally clairalience. The first claircognance, is the knowledge of future events, knowing intuitively what is going to happen without any prior knowledge about the situation. Some people call this a gut feeling. The second clairvoyant awareness, is seeing in your mind's eye a future event, or images and messages from spirit in the form of pictures. Mediums are using this sense along with their physical eyes when they see spirit. When I see spirits, they appear and disappear with the blink of an eye. It is very fast and easy to miss, but after seeing the spirit with my physical eyes, my clairvoyant sense kicks in and takes over and I begin to receive images in my mind's eye from spirit. The third is clairsentient awareness. This sense allows the medium to feel the physical sensations the spirit felt before passing. Along with the emotions the spirit wants to communicate to the living. This is how mediums can receive specifics about how a person passed into spirit. One example of this, I was reading for a woman who's loved one had passed from cancer. Prior to passing this individual had to consume many medications. When I connected with this woman's spirit, I got the sensation of being nauseous and was shown the inside of a hospital room. If I had only been shown the inside of the hospital room, I may not have been able to validate for my client that I was connecting with the proper individual. Many situations occur inside the setting of a hospital room. Operations, broken bones, births, deaths, heart attacks. I could of come to the conclusion that this individual had been part of the medical profession during life. This is a good example of when two or more types of psychic awareness are needed to work together to help validate the proper information. The fourth clairaudience, hearing inner or outer thoughts that are from spirit. This can be very subtle and is not one of my stronger psychic senses. During a reading I rarely receive the name of the individual I'm connecting with. When I begin a reading, I dive right into the details the spirit is showing me rather than trying to figure out what their name was during their life time here on earth. Many mediums have a better clairaudient sense and can hear names better than myself. For me personally it is just a waste of my time, and the clients time. There are two additional senses. They are clairgustance (clear tasting) and clairalience(clear smelling). With clairgustance, the medium may taste a favorie food, or possibly like with the nauseous feeling, get a bitter taste in the mouth. Clairalience happens quite often. When my grandfather visits he brings the smell of cigar smoke along with him. I think many of us have had that moment, they swear they can smell the inside of their grandparents home, or their grandmother's baking. However brief those moments might be, they are real signs that our loved ones soul is in our presence. Spirit is very subtle with the signs they send us and these signs can be very easily overlooked. Often what we imagine a sign from spirit might be, is just not realistic to have happen here in our physical world. The spiritual world is working at such a higher and faster vibration than the physical world, which is why the information from spirit comes at us so fast, and is so easy for us to miss. Our loved ones who have crossed over into the world of spirit are sending us signs each and every day. The best way to notice these signs is when the mind is quiet, and we can be calm and concentrate. Mediums often miss important details because the information is bombarding the medium and all of her senses at an extremely fast rate of speed. There are times when I am connecting to spirit I feel as if I just consumed twenty cups of coffee. The energy is so strong and so fast at times my hands will tremble and sweat. I urge anyone who desires to connect with the other side on their own, to first practice meditation. Meditation is by far the best way to calm and quiet the waking mind and body so that you are able to connect with spirit.

Every reading is a learning experience. Most messages are straight forward, but some are not. Some mediums will always receive the same symbols for each reading, for example being shown a certain color flower will always symbolize an upcoming anniversary etc. I will not always receive the same symbols and mine for the most part are straightforward. Spirit will just show me a scene from their life, or I will feel their emotions. I'm not quite sure why different mediums have different styles of reading and connecting with the other side. I feel spirit conforms to each mediums unique personality. I myself am very direct in my personal life, almost a little to blunt at times. The whole concept of reading between the lines goes out the window with me. Spirit knows this and just throws everything out on the table. In the end the message is what matters no matter what style of communication a medium brings to the reading. Even though I feel spirit is direct with communicating with me, each reading, every life experience, each spirit that is trying to communicate, is as individual as we are.

It has also been my experience that some clients are easier to read than others. I'm not sure why that is. At times we have a spirit come through and the client has no idea who they are because they personally didn't know them while they were living. And there are times when a client only wants to hear from a particular loved one who has passed and just doesn't want to hear anything else. It is so important to keep an open mind to all of the information that is coming through during a reading. There is always a chance another family member can confirm the information for you after the reading is over.

It has been a long spiritual journey for myself to get to a point in my life where I am truly at ease and confident in my abilities as a psychic medium. I now can finally see and understand the purpose of the events from my past that left me wondering what the point in all of it was. I am now so very grateful to have the opportunity to bring a smile of comfort to those who come to me looking for answers. It warms my heart to be able to help others in such a profound way.

Chapter Two

Spirit Guides

Every single one of us has a spirit guide in tow whether we like it or not. Spirit guides are with us all the time all day every day their job is to help us through life's mud and muck it doesn't matter to them if we notice they're existence or not. Our guides know exactly how to use our intuition to help us avoid accidents, or dangerous situations. That feeling you may get when you meet someone that there is something not right with that person, you feel they might be harmful or they just seem creepy, that's your guide whispering in your ear, nudging you to not trust that situation or person.

Spirit guides are very different from angels. The most important difference is that angels have never lived a life as a human but spirit guides have. Our guides can be someone we knew and shared a past life with. Or an ancestor that passed before we were born. Before we are born into our present life, both souls agree on who will be your guide. Your guide will also know of your life's plan as you are mapping out your trials and tribulations. Guides cannot stop every bad situation from happening in your life. We need these situations to happen so that our souls can grow and learn spiritually. Our guides are there to give us the inner strength we need to keep fighting during the hard emotional times. Those horrible situations where you have no idea how you found the strength to keep going, you guide was there. Angels will come and assist you as well, wrapping their loving protective wings around your soul. The difference being, angels will come and go, but your guide is there from the moment you take your first precious tear filled breath, until the day you joyfully return home to the other side.

One experience I had with my guide whispering in my ear to warn me of impending danger happened when I was 19 and still in my bubble so to speak. I was driving home from a babysitting job, from which I always took the same route home. It made me feel safer, ha! "Something" persistent was telling me to take an alternate route home. Well I wrestled with my best friend a.ka. Anxiety and finally gave in and drove home using a different route. As I was approaching the intersection I noticed the flashing lights of a police car. There had been an accident right where my little Chevy sprint would have been. And yeah I would have been toast! That feeling that wouldn't stop was my guide whispering in my ear. Our guides will use our intuition and psychic senses to communicate with us.

Our guides will communicate with us in very subtle ways. Most of us have had that moment when we are not really thinking about much in particular and suddenly you have a revelation about a serious issue in your life. That is you guide helping you, giving you the information you need at that moment in your life. I call these light bulb moments "pops". I have never heard the voice of my guide with my physical ear. For myself it's a pop, or a feeling that something is not right.

I have had one experience with seeing her. I was desperately feeling the need to have an encounter with the being I have felt by side for as long as I could remember. Every night before I drifted off to sleep, I asked her in my mind's eye, not really knowing who to imagine in front of me, I could not really get a mental picture so it was like I was asking that familiar presence I knew, to please show herself to me. Of course I was expecting to have one of my vivid dreams where we would meet each other on the other side and we would prance through beautiful fields of flowers smiling with the bright warm light of home shining bliss upon us. But the reality was much different. One night shortly after asking to see her, I awoke suddenly out of a sound sleep, to see her standing at the foot of the bed! As quickly as she was there she was gone but I instantly knew it was her. She was a beautiful woman in her 30's with long curly auburn hair, with big expressive beautiful eyes that were the same unique color as her hair. She was wearing a long flowing white robe that looked like something worn in ancient Greek or Roman times. She was also wearing a white headpiece. She glowed with the pure white light and love of the other side. The love I felt emanating from her was indescribable, I wish I could of bottled it up and kept it so I could feel it again. It was a feeling of unconditional love, peace, and acceptance.

I communicate with my guide during meditations, and when my mind is still or "blank". I have always been able to very easily get to the alpha state, which for myself is like daydreaming. So in essence, I will begin to day dream or sometimes I call it zoning out and that's when I will receive my pops from my guide. I get into this state during a reading as well. There are times when I desire to be in a deeper meditative state. For this I need to be alone, eyes shut, so that I can receive visions as well as answers to my questions. My mind can drift into the alpha state, while I'm talking with someone, watching television, or reading.

My guide has shared with me and shown me images of home. I will try to describe what I have been shown. I know there are no words that can do the beauty and peace of the other side justice. There are beautiful cascading waterfalls, that create the most wondrous sound when the water flows from the top and hit's the surface below. There are the most beautifully constructed temples of gold and buildings that are constructed like the ancient Greek and Roman buildings and temples. There also exists, pyramids, and buildings like those of ancient Babylon. All of the ancient wonders and structures of the world are replicas of buildings that existed first on the other side. This is also true of our modern day sky scrapers. On the other side these structures are even more awe inspiring then they are here. The buildings and temples here on the earth plane are but ant hills by comparison. We re create these structures because our souls long for the beauty and peace that exists on the other side.

Animals live in harmony with us at home. There is no need for violence between the species. That is why as humans we long for animal companionship and imagine we can have a relationship with a wild animal here on earth. This is how the concept of pet ownership evolved here on the earth plane. Our souls remember our animal companions of every shape and size on the other side. The most beautiful gardens fill the other side with the sweetest flowery smells you could imagine. Our souls long for the immense beauty of home and we try to re create it here on the earth plane. The earth is but a dim reflection of home. Take the most picturesque seen you have ever seen and magnify that by thousands, that is the beauty of home. The only emotions that exist at home are peace, love, understanding, and acceptance. That is the reason most of us strive for that here on earth.

The earth plane is a negative plane, that is our souls struggle, to experience the negativity here on earth and grow spiritually from it. Babies and children are so innocent because they just arrived here from home. As we grow, the soul is reminded of the negative aspects here. The veil that exists between us and home, consists of pure negative energy. It is our souls mission here on earth as humans to create peace on this earth, and remove it from its negative state. There is a darkness that needs to go. Only the bravest of souls choose to live a life here on space ship earth. Our mission as humans is to bring peace and light to this hell that earth has become.

Our guides try their best to warn us when we need help. At times they may use our pets to assist them. Animals are naturally intuitive and are not affected by the negative "vibes" that permeate the earth plane, as much as humans are. They can nudge our animal companions into action when they cannot get our attention. The dog that loves everyone, but there is that one individual he always growls at or won't go anywhere near, that is your warning to stay away or be cautious around that individual. This is also true for service animals. A service animal that performs an incredible feat to save it's unconscious owner, is being guided and directed by its owners spirit guide. Animals are more receptive to telepathic messages. Dogs that eventually become guide dogs, are even more receptive than the average dog. They intuitively know what their person needs and how to keep them safe. Our pets were given to us as a gift to make life more enjoyable.

If you are wanting to connect with your guide, start by asking silently for your guide to come to you in a way that is comfortable for you. I asked mine to show herself during the dream state because I thought it would less intimidating that way, apparently she thought I could handle seeing her form on this plane. Ask for what you feel comfortable with. Practice paying attention to those light bulb moments. The moments of clarity where things suddenly make sense, the more attention you pay to these moments, the better your communication with your guide will be. I also recommend keeping a journal to record these moments, this will help you recognize the "style" in which your guide communicates with you. Ultimately, the best and most effective way to meet and communicate with your guide, is through meditation. It will take practice depending on how easy it is for you to relax, but it is worth it in the long run.

Our guides are always here for us and will love us unconditionally no matter what choices we make here on earth, until the day we joyfully cross over and return home to the other side. I wanted to share some of my spirit guide pops with you. The following are some that helped answer some questions I had about life, religion, and relationships.

I was pondering the question of why there are so many different religions here on earth. This was my answer "Perception is in the eye of the beholder." "Meaning there are as many religious truths as there are human beings. Everyone perceives what they hear and see in their own unique way. Two people sitting next to each other in church listening to the same sermon are not going to have the exact same interpretation of what is being said. The reverend will not be able to convey the message the exact way it was meant to be interpreted when it was written. This is a constant among all religions. We are drawn to a religion based upon who or what spiritual being trained our guide before we were born, based on what life we chose to live out before we return here. The beautiful temples described previously are where some of the spirit guide training takes place. Jesus trains guides in a beautifully constructed temple of gold. Buddha trains in a temple with beautiful gardens. Some guides get the pleasure of being trained by the Goddess herself. Guides, whose humans have chosen a particularly harder lives than others, will receive more intense and a longer training period, but both souls will have learned and grown immensely from these difficult life lessons." Some other pops were "I am your inner strength in a world of turmoil." and "live by the golden rule." At a time in my life when I had questions about forgiveness this was her answer. " It is not necessary to forgive those who have caused you emotional or physical pain. It is possible to move on and grow and learn from the experience, the lesson almost always being strength and understanding, without forgiveness. True forgiveness can only come from God(s)." "We choose every situation we encounter here on earth before we are born, even the most horrific, painful, struggles we choose them for our souls journey. God will not let us choose any tragedy our souls can not handle. Only the bravest, strongest souls choose the hardest struggles. The end result for us all, is love, peace, acceptance and soul growth." She also says " Our higher self is simply our subconscious mind. Everything we need to know lies within our subconscious mind." "Some of us can tap into that mind, some can not, simply because they do not need to at his moment." When I was wondering about the universe and possible life forms on other planets, this is the response I got. "When we gaze at the night sky we are looking at home that is home the stars, the sky, the planets, are other planes of existence . Time is the barrier we cannot break through to reach them, time is infinite that is the infinite wisdom of home." "Science is God personified." I was wondering about life energy how it interacts with the physical body. She replied with, " Life is energy it changes, looses speed, speeds up, enters new forms, leaves old forms, never dies. The form it leaves behind has been changed by its experience with the energy and vice-versa The shell form it leaves behind, lives on in a different physical form as it gives life to the earth it collapses on. Any given living being here on earth is essentially two different energy forms intermingling with each other until they separate, the spiritual energy goes on home to the spiritual plane, the physical body, changes its energy to keep the physical plane alive." The next message I'm not entirely sure where she was going with it or why exactly it popped in my head. We were driving home from shopping listening to the radio and in it popped. I feel she does want me to share, but I think we need a Biblical scholar to interpret this one. " Jesus and Mary Magdelene were brother and sister." Now don't shoot the messenger! But it would explain why they never got together romantically.

Communicating with your guide is a unique and uplifting experience. Whether we connect with them or not, they are there looking out for you, ready to be your strength in your time of need.

Chapter Three

Ghosts

Everyone who has had experiences with the paranormal, that I have come across says without question that there exists more than one type of ghost. There is the confused ghost that has no idea that's its soul has left its physical body, and then there is the ghost that chooses to stay because it is afraid or does not want to cross over, and the ghosts of children. When the soul leaves the physical body, it is leaving whatever physical or mental state it suffered behind with the physical body that has ceased to function. The soul leaves, and is back to its natural spiritual state. Therefore the soul is always fully aware when it is no longer alive, in a physical body. Any soul that does not cross over, and stays behind here on earth, does so by its own choice.

Then there is the issue of the ghosts of innocent children wandering helplessly where they passed on for an eternity. The spirit world is not that cruel. We all have a guide to help our souls when we leave our physical form, also the soul that is occupying that child's body is not necessarily a young soul when it leaves the body. The soul always knows when it has left a physical form. When people witness a ghost in child form, they are not seeing ghosts, they are seeing the spirit of the deceased soul. When a spirit visit's a place it may of lived, people will see them the age they were when they passed. There are no souls of children that get left behind.

Ghosts appear as black shadowy figures and often you can't tell what that person looked like before they passed. There are many reasons why a soul might decide to stay behind and not return home. Some stay to wreak havoc on the earth plane because they are negative energies. Some stay waiting for a loved one to join them. Some stay because they were murdered and want to torment the person who took their life, or to see justice served. Others stay because they do not want to face the judgment for their evil acts here on earth. Ghosts stay here on earth because they want to. They always have the choice to cross over whenever they want. The door to the other side is always open to every soul who has left it's physical form.

The worst experience I have ever had with a ghost was at my mother's home in Falmouth, Massachusetts. I was staying with her temporarily while I was divorcing my first husband. It began with seeing shadowy movement from the corner of my eye, and hearing my name called by a male voice when I was home alone. When I was in the home, I was constantly tired. More than my normal tiredness. I have always had the tendency to get tired easily, and I guess you could say I am a low energy person, but all I wanted to do while I was there was sleep. I also experienced very bad moods, from depression, to just plain being angry for no apparent reason. I would notice as soon as I stepped over the threshold, my mood would change from happy or neutral, to downright furious for no reason. One night when I was laying in bed upstairs, I kept seeing a black shadowy figure next to the bed with my per phial vision. I mentioned what I was seeing and we decided to try and communicate with it. Not a wise idea. I grabbed my notebook and pen and we began asking questions. The first sensation I noticed was a hot spot directly in front of my face. Then I felt the entity get very close to me and invade my personal space. In the moments that followed my boyfriend and I proceeded to have the worst argument of our relationship. I felt a wave of hate come over me, and I proceeded to call him every name in the book! The next morning when I woke up, it was like nothing had happened. I recalled the argument, but not the intensity of it. I want to state although negative entity's like this one can influence people to become angry, under no circumstances do I believe an entity can possess someone's physical form and force them to harm another person. Or influence a person to the point where they commit murder.

I learned from this awful experience to never try and communicate with a negative energy without first protecting myself with white light. I did not properly prepare myself by making sure my aura was protected. This entity took full advantage of my eagerness to communicate with it. Now I tell negative energies to leave my space, ignore them completely, which they hate, or burn sage while commanding them to leave. When I started asking questions and acknowledged the entity's presence, I gave it the fuel it needed for its fire that night.

I wouldn't want to be the new owner's of that home. While we were living there we would constantly be burning sage, and performing banishing rituals, when we felt the energy take a turn for the worse. Things would quiet down for a bit but he always returned. At one point we set up a digital recorder to try and capture a voice or any other evidence on audio. We captured a male voice mumbling but couldn't make out what exactly he was saying. My last experience with the entity before we moved, happened in the living room on the first floor. We were all camped out in front of the television. I was still a little shaken by our argument and didn't want to sleep upstairs. All of the lights were out except for the light from the television screen. Once again I saw the shadowy movement out of the corner of my eye. I was scared, and of course everyone else was sound asleep. I slowly turned my head toward the shadowy figure, and there he was right in front of me, the darkest black darker than the darkness, humanoid figure. I tried to wake up my better half but as soon as I worked up the words, the shadow disappeared before my eyes.

There are some people who have encountered nasty energies that say they have been hurt physically by them. Spirits and ghosts can touch and poke us lightly. They can not push, or punch us. People that report these incidents are telling the truth about getting hurt but it's not the entity that hurt them. Most likely it is their first experience with a nasty energy, they hear or see something that frightens them, they jump or trip, and inadvertently hurt themselves.

This was the worst haunting I ever experienced but not the first. The first haunting I experienced occurred at my grandparent's home in Plymouth Massachusetts. The house had an uneasy feeling about it, and there was an overwhelming energy of a "grumpy" man that permeated the house, with the heaviest concentration coming from the upper level of the home. I dreaded the long climb up the old wooden stair case, to use the bathroom upstairs. There was a small room at the top of the stairs I had to pass by, that as long as I could remember remained empty. I was drawn to and repelled by the energy of that room. I recall standing at the threshold staring into the room and feeling the male presence radiating from the room like a burst of bright sunlight. Needless to say I never worked up the courage to step foot into that room. The house was built in the early 1900's and I'm sure held plenty of history.

Dealing with a negative energy is never an easy task. Ghosts will not leave what they consider to be there space until they are ready to. It is possible to lighten the energy of a haunted space and make living a little easier until the entity decides to leave. If you're not comfortable doing this yourself, have someone else come in and clear the energy for you. And never try and communicate with a negative being without first protecting your aura with the white light of home.

I have found the most effective way of clearing negative energy, whether it be ghostly energy, or negative psychic energy, for example you just had a nasty argument with a loved one, this can leave behind residual, nasty psychic energy, is by purifying your space with sage smoke. The use of smoke to purify and spiritually cleanse an area has been used for thousands of years by many ancient cultures. Ancient Hindu's used this method six thousand years ago using the smoke from incense. Also the ancient cultures of Rome, Greece, and Egypt all used smoke purification rituals as a part of their religious ceremonies. Native Americans use sage and other sacred plants in their smoke purification rituals. I use white sage(Salvia Apiana) found at the coastal mountain regions of California. The sage smoke purifies the energy of a space when the smoke attaches itself to the negative energy and clears it by taking the negative energy with it out away from your space.

There are different ways sage can be bought, either as a bundle or loose leaf. I prefer the loose leaf because I can burn it in a ceramic bowl, it's a little easier to control where exactly the smoke goes, and I don't need to be concerned with falling embers. When using a smudge stick or bundle, often times as you are walking, movement can cause loose embers to fall on the floor or your clothes.

Before you begin your smudging, clean the area, pick things up put everything in its proper place, clean and organize whatever needs to be put away. Clear the area of as many physical objects as you can. Make your self comfortable in the room where you are going to begin your smudging. Close your eyes, relax your muscles, take one or two deep breathes, exhaling all the tension your body is carrying. Then envision yourself protected by the white light of home. First surrounding you then radiating outward, until it fills the room, and eventually the entire home, then the outside of your home until it is completely enveloped in the pure loving protective white light of home. Say a prayer either to your self or out loud which ever makes you most comfortable, to the higher power you feel is your protector. I ask Archangel Michael when I smudge. Ask your spiritual protector to protect and clear you, your loved ones, and your home of any and all negative energies that are present. Light the sage and carry it through each room. Let the smoke purify each room. You only need to walk in and around the perimeter of the room, but if you want to spend more time in a room that's acceptable as well. When you feel each room has been smudged to your liking simply extinguish the sage according to the directions it came with.

I always tell people you can never smudge to often. I smudge at least twice a week to keep the energies of my home balanced. Even if you are smudging on a regular basis, you still should go ahead and smudge if you start to feel uncomfortable.

Another tool I use to handle negative energies is salt. It can be table salt or sea salt. I sprinkle it in the corners of a room, let it do its job, and clean it up after its been there three days. You can also sprinkle it on doorways and window sills, or outside the perimeter of your home to keep the nasty energy out. I keep a small bowl of salt out on my book shelf and change it every three days. The salt works by absorbing any negative energy that is present.

White candles also do a really good job clearing your space of negative energy. The color white is symbolic of the loving protective energy of the divine. When lit the energy of the flame disperses the negative energy out away from the area. This works even better when blessed with holy water. I simply take holy water I gathered from a church and dab it on the candle before I burn it. You can also carve a protective word into the candle before burning it.

Lastly holy water is also a very effective tool to use to squash the negative energies that might be roaming about. Sprinkle it anywhere and everywhere you feel comfortable. I put a dab on my forehead (third eye). And of course holy water works so well because it has been blessed by a religious figure.

I use all of these methods together but they can be used separately as well. I also call on the help of Archangel Michael to protect me. I visualize Archangel Michael using his sword to "cut" negative energy away from me, and to form a protective barrier around my aura. I visualize Michael either in front of me or above me, with the white light of home extending outward from his sword and surrounding my aura with loving protective energy.

Where ghosts are concerned it is very important to ignore their energy as much as you can. When you notice their presence flicking lights, making knocking noises, or being an annoying shadowy figure, stay calm. Pretend not to notice ignore them as you would a toddler throwing a tantrum. They hate being ignored because they feed off your fear and become a bigger presence this way. When you ignore them which is not easy when you first discover you have a haunting, they become bored and calm down, which in turn calms the energy of the home as well. Please remember they cannot physically hurt you this will help you keep your calm. Although no ghost will leave until it wants to, if you happen to have a nasty ghost that's hanging around for the purpose of wreaking havoc and scaring people ignoring really can do wonders for the problem and might help the negative energy decide to finally pack up it's suit case and go home.

Spirit Attachments

A spirit attachment is said to occur when a dark or negative energy attaches itself to a person's aura. This is done by the entity to cause physical and or psychological harm to an individual. First there is a major difference between spirits and dark or negative energies. Spirits are always positive, loving beings of light and do not have ill intentions toward living beings. Ghosts and dark energies on the other hand, want nothing more than to scare and disturb people's lives. That being said, in order to discuss the topic we first need to re-name it from spirit attachment to ghost or dark energy attachment. Dark energies do exist. Dark energies can make us feel fear, put us in grumpy mood, make us tired, snippy, and depressed. Now when I say depressed I mean within a normal range, not to the point of giving up on life. Dark energies are able to do this when they get to close to your aura, not by attaching to it. That is the very reason we have auras in the first place. Auras act as a natural protective barrier against attachments, and being entered by a dark energy. Auras will not allow a dark energy to enter a person's physical form. Dark energies are always attached to places. They cannot attach to living beings. The only time they can affect our mood is when you are in a haunted building or on haunted land. Places are haunted not people. You should be aware of negative energies but not afraid. They feed of our fear of them and that is what they enjoy.

Remember ghost stories as shown on television and in Hollywood movies is not reality. And these stories that may be based on true events, are greatly exaggerated to sell tickets and sometimes books. If you find yourself in the company of an un wanted ghost, stay calm and be assured it will not harm you.

Chapter Four

Astral Travel and Dreams

Since the beginning of time human beings have been fascinated by dreams. Where do they come from? What happens in our minds when we adventure through random stories during our slumber. The first known written record of dream interpretation and meanings was found in ancient Egypt on the Chester Beaty papyrus dating back to 1350 B.C. The ancient Egyptians believed the Goddess Bes was responsible for the night time story line of dreams.

Dreams were a sacred part of Egyptian culture. So sacred that temple priests who were dream interpreters were called "Masters of the Secret Things." The priests received their knowledge by studying the "Book of the Dead" a book of ancient Egyptian wisdom. It was their believe that the gods revealed themselves in dreams. It was also believed that dreams gave warnings, advice, and prophecies. The ancient Egyptians belief in knowledge gained through dreams was so strong that the written symbol representing the word dream, was of an open eye.

There is also evidence that the ancient Egyptians also developed an advanced practice of conscious dream travel. Trained dreamers worked as seers, telepaths, and at times remote viewers. The remote viewers were said to aid military strategies.

Yet another ancient culture that took the study of dreams to a new level was ancient Greece. It was there that a Greek living in the fourth century, wrote the first known book of dreams. Antiphon created the book to be used for dream interpretation. Unlike the ancient Egyptians, Antiphon believed that dreams did not come from the gods or the spiritual realm, but are born of the subconscious. The believe that dreams could predict the future events and contain psychic messages was still held by some. In second century A.D. a book of dream meanings was written by Artemidorus, a Greek physician who was living in Rome. Artemidorus placed dreams into specific categories in order to describe them. They were, dreams, visions, oracles, fantasies, and apparitions. Prophetic dreams were called somnium, and insomnium dreams were simply random nightly story lines. It was for the somnium that Artemidorus created the dream dictionary. Artemidorus also maintained that a persons name, nationality, and social status, influenced the meaning of their night time dreams. Yet another ancient Greek, Aristides, is responsible for writing the first dream diary during the time period of 530 to 468 BC. It was titled The Sacred Teachings. It was an enormous work of five volumes. He titled his work the Sacred Teachings because a large number of the dreams he recorded were about Aesculapius, the god of healing. He described how the god Aesculapius taught him in his dreams how to cure illnesses.

Thousands of miles away across the Atlantic Ocean Native American tribes were dreaming their dreams, and holding them sacred. In Native American culture, dreams are treated with great respect and used as a means for gathering sacred wisdom and guidance for life. It is believed that visits from ancestors and animal spirits, the dreamers totem animal, held significant meanings. Woven into almost every Native tribes beliefs, was that everyone had a dream spirit that watched over every dreamer and would be of help to each dreamer. One of these sacred spirits was the white deer. Native Americans respect all animal life, and when an animal dies, a prayer is said over the animal and no part of the animal is wasted. The dream spirit of the white deer helps guide the dreamer to an action or destination. It was taught that if the dreamer dreamed of the white wolf it was a warning that there is a danger nearby that the dreamer has overlooked. The following quote is an excellent example of the importance of dreams in Native American culture. The quote is from White Hair, a medicine man. "Every dream that takes place is certain to happen. Whenever the evil spirits influence it, it is certain to happen. Whenever we dream a bad dream we get a medicine man to perform sing and say prayers which will banish the spirit." It was also tradition for natives to seek wisdom and guidance through vision quests. Men of any age could embark on a vision quest, but it was also a rite of passage for young males. Young people or those seeking a vision for the first time, were accompanied by a medicine person. The ritual began with a sweat bath, in a small hut, where his mind and physical being would be purified by the hot steam. The steam was created by continuously pouring water over extremely hot stones. He then traveled to an isolated place, and got a sacred spot ready. Then would fast and pray for many days until he connected with the spirit of the earth and sky. Not until he fully connected would he have his vision that would contain the answers he was seeking. The great chief Sitting Bull went on several vision quests throughout his lifetime. It was during a vision quest that he saw ranks of mounted soldiers approaching the village. Sitting bull predicted his village would be attacked by the Calvary, but would survive and his people would win a great victory. Three weeks later, at the famous battle of Little Bighorn, the natives wiped out Custer's army with little casualties on their side. I can't help but wonder how many other of Sitting Bull's visions were realized.

Now we journey back over the Atlantic one last time to peer into the mystical and magical lands of the Celts. In this land Dream time is the place where everyone existed before time. Dream time is the place of thought and spirit and the beginning of everything. A place just as real as the physical world. It was believed that dreaming opened the door into the land of the fae, and that our nightly dreams always contained prophecies. In the tale of Angus Mac Og, while young Angus slept, a beautiful faery woman showed herself to him. When he woke up, he could think of nothing except for this beautiful faery woman who came to him in his dreams. He looked for her for a year until he finally found her, all the while she kept appearing to him every night in his dreams.

The belief that our nightly dreams contained prophecies and visits from the gods, and our deceased loved ones, was common place, at least for the ancient world. I believe the ancients must of observed some validations after dreaming, for this belief to be so prevalent across a wide range of cultures, cultures that would not meet each other for centuries to come.

Modern science knows that sleep is the body's way to rest and restore energy levels. A good night's sleep is essential to deal with stress, resolve problems, and stay healthy. Sleep is controlled by natural cycles of activity in the brain. There are two basic states of sleep, rapid eye movement and non rapid eye movement. During the night the brain and body cycle between these two stages of sleep, with most of our dreams occurring during the rapid eye movement stage. Modern science knows why we sleep but not why we dream. While numerous theories have been thrown about, why we dream is still a scientific mystery. Some researchers say that dreams serve no real purpose while others say that dreaming is essential to emotional and mental, and physical well being. Some of the scientific theories suggest that dreams are the result of our brains trying to make sense of external stimuli that is happening around us while we are sleeping. We incorporate the sounds we hear into what we are dreaming about. Yet another theory is that dreams are the minds way of working through our daily problems, solving them, and getting us ready for the upcoming day. The fact remains that the scientific community has no idea what dreams are or how they function. Dreams have been studied by humans for centuries and from the spiritual side of the coin there is no doubt what they are, messages from the world of spirit. I will say however that not every dream is a message or a visitation from the other side. Some are simply random stories or scary subconscious fears playing themselves out. But the fact remains that the spiritual evidence and evidence of the prophetic dream is more logical than the present scientific answer of "We have no idea."

I personally have gathered many notes over the years detailing my prophetic dreams. It's simple, I have a dream or vision of a future event, it happens no other explanation is needed at least not for me. I have always had amazing dream recall, and very vivid dreams. The prophetic dreams even more detailed and vivid then my normal dreams. Almost as real as what my waking mind experiences, it's as if I am actually there having the experience, feeling physical pain and all the emotions. I experience it as the person I'm dreaming about in their body. Something else that happens with my dreams, I am able to "script" my dreams. If I wake up during a pleasant dream, I can close my eyes and pick up where I leave off. This also happens during prophetic dreams if I am woken up, but its not under my control at that time. A lot of my prophetic dreams are about tragic events and personally I do not want to finish those events. My prophetic dreams are accurate, but at times I misinterpret the meaning. An excellent example of that was a dream I had about hurricane Sandy about six months before it happened.

In the dream I was standing in the middle of Central Park. I was holding a baby girl, when suddenly the sky turned gray, the earth started to shake, and big trees started toppling over. I could feel the earth beneath me shake as the huge trees hit the ground. I felt the fear of others around me and my own as people were running and screaming. When I woke up, I interpreted the dream as meaning New York City was going to have a major earth quake. I think the fear and emotion I felt kept me from reviewing the vision, if I had I believe I would of took into account the overcast gray sky. In the days following Sandy, some of the photos I saw on the news looked like what I saw in my vision. I believe my vision was completely accurate, but I interpreted it wrong, because it was so vivid I didn't want to keep reliving it to figure it out.

Amazing experiences can happen to us in our dream state including visits from the people we love who are now living in the glory of the other side. Anyone can visit with loved ones who have crossed over while in the dream state. If you are someone who remembers their dreams easily then this should not be difficult. I think we do not always remember these visitations from spirit simply because we are not excepting them, and we forget when we wake up. A good way to remember your nightly dreams, is as soon as you wake up, go over the dreams you remember having and if you have time, write down everything you remember even if it seems like nonsense. At different points during the day remind yourself of the dreams you had the night before and think about them. This will strengthen your ability to recall your dreams. I do this every day partly out of habit, partly as a reminder to keep my abilities strong. Most important, believe your loved one will come to you, leave every doubt at the door and embrace the fact that you will have a visitation with every fiber of your being. As you are drifting off to sleep ask your loved one to come to you. Ask your guide, God, whoever you feel comfortable with to bring them fourth. Think of a happy time you had with your loved one and picture them there with you in your mind's eye. It might take some practice, but it will happen. There are times when it is to soon and you may have to wait simply because the pain is still too deep. When my maternal grandmother passed it took over ten years for her to visit me in the dream state, and I'm a medium! They will come when they know you can handle seeing them again. When it does it such a beautiful experience you will have no doubt the visit was real. One night I had a visitation from my paternal grandmother that was so real I asked her if I had passed away in my sleep. She just smirked at me and shook her head no. She was in her 80's when she passed but when I was with her at that moment she was young and vibrant, happy, with no trace of any illness. I have had visitations with my paternal grandparents, my maternal grandmother, and my cousin a few weeks before I found out the sad news that she had passed. It was actually that visitation that led me to contact my father's sister who I hadn't spoken with for several years. And she told me what had happened. Also keep in mind where you are having the visitation in the dream. A dream of the other side will be filled with bright colors, and beautiful imagery. The colors will be the easiest to notice, they make the most vibrant, bright colors of earth appear black and white.

Although you are dreaming of the other side, and being visited by the spirit of a loved one, you and your soul are not actually there, you stay comfy in your bed. Your loved one comes to you and telepathically communicates with you. It is so easy for the majority of us to have visitations during sleep, because in order to communicate with the other side, the brain needs to be in the Alpha state. This state occurs naturally as part of the sleep process. Mediums like myself can reach the Alpha state while awake.

Astral travel is a much different experience then dreaming. It is not the same as normal dreaming, or lucid dreaming. Astral travel occurs when your soul or astral body travels outside of your physical body. Astral travel is what is occurring when people use remote viewing to gather information. You can not travel a far distance away from your physical body. You need to stay close to you physical body while astral traveling. Your soul or astral form is connected by what some call a silver cord. I perceive this as simply a connection of energy in the form of a cord that keeps your soul from completely detaching from your physical body so that you don't cross over. The cord is a piece of your soul or astral form that stretches like an elastic band, but it can only stretch so far, and astral travel is limited by this constraint.

Your soul or astral form travels around the physical plane while astral traveling. You can not visit the other side while in astral form because you will crossover, even though you are attached by the cord, you can not visit the other side while in this astral form. You can gather spiritual information and messages while in astral form, but like with dreaming, the information comes to you, you do not go to it.

From the time I was a young child I have had several astral travel experiences. I have no control over when it happens. It does seem to occur more often in the spring and summer months. It never happens while I'm awake, it occurs at night when my body is sleeping, or at times when I am napping. So now how do I know I'm astral traveling and not dreaming? Well aside from my intuitive knowing, these experiences are extremely vivid, I think I get up out of bed, walk around talk to loved ones, if they are not sleeping. For example if I happen to be napping, I believe I wake up walk out of the bedroom and have a conversation with someone. One problem though they don't notice me there. When I'm finished traveling I return to my sleeping body, and what follows is a sleep paralysis experience where I'm awake in my body, but my body will not budge. I have to calm my mind before my eyes open. When I wake up it takes me a few moments to realize I'm actually awake. The astral travel experiences that happen during the night are slightly different. I never remember the act of leaving my body, with any astral experience. It's not until I'm traveling that I notice. When I was a child I would travel from my bedroom, into the living room, where we had a large picture window. My astral self would gaze up at the night sky. As I'm watching the night sky, out of nowhere about a dozen little yellow balls of gold light appear in the sky. They turn what was a black sky into a cobalt blue colored sky with their beautiful glow. I watch as they twist and turn and speed around in the sky. They dance around in the night for a bit then suddenly start to spell out messages sent just for me. I wish I could remember now what they said, but I have no doubt they were filled with what I needed to know at that time in my young life. Other astral travel incidents consisted of traveling outside to my backyard, and a bright light glowing on me from above, as I look down there was a rabbit at my feet.

There was a time when I was around eight or nine, one of my older brothers pointed out circles that had been pressed into the grass outside my bedroom window. I can't say for certain they appeared after an astral travel event, but its interesting to note. Most of my astral travel experiences have been uneventful. My little yellow ball of light friends, have not returned since I was about nine. Now they consist of a walk around the home or maybe a quick journey out to the yard. I do not enjoy astral traveling. I dislike the feeling of it, it's not fearful until I re-enter my body and feel the discomfort of sleep paralysis. I have no control over when it happens that I'm aware of, and I have never actively tried to astral travel on my own. I do not believe it is a dangerous event to try and accomplish, maybe if I actively took control I could combat the sleep paralysis, I'm not sure. But, I am including some information here on different astral travel techniques for those who are interested. What I am adding is basic information do give a better understanding of what an astral travel experience is like. I recommend researching as much as possible before trying to astral travel on your own.

First you must be relaxed as possible, in mind and body. I recommend mastering some mediation techniques in order to achieve the required state of relaxation. Experiment with different ways of traveling, what works for one person may be difficult for another. A popular method is called the rope method. You visualize yourself climbing out of your body with the help of a rope. With another method you simply visualize yourself floating freely outside your body. Yet another method has the traveler visualize a solid object pulling your astral form free from your physical body. There is no wrong or right time of day to astral travel practice at different times during the day to find out which works best for you. As you are leaving your physical body you might feel some paralysis. It isn't something to fear, but as I said this is why I personally do not enjoy astral travel, so make sure you are aware this sensation can happen, but at the same time, it can't harm you and only lasts a few seconds. It can occur as you are leaving, and returning, I only recall it happening when I re-enter my physical form. Also remember you will stay close to your body, and are always attached to the silver cord, so you will not crossover or get lost on the astral plane. Like with dreaming of a loved one who has crossed, you must believe and have the intent that you are without a doubt going to astral travel. I feel it is also a great idea to journal your experiences, to discover the best techniques that work for you, and also what goodies you might learn while traveling. Psychic information comes to you, you do not go to it, so asking before you astral project is never a bad idea. You will also be spiritually protected but if it makes you feel more at ease ask a guide, an angel, a passed loved one, to protect you during your travels. There is also the technique of visualizing the bright white light of home around you, this will always protect you.

The most amazing experiences can happen for us during our night time sleep. We can sometimes see the future, and have a loving encounter with a loved one who has crossed over. The astral travel experience can be remarkably similar, but so very different at the same time.

If we take control of our dreams and our possible soul travels, we can open up a whole new world of experiences, and evidence that our souls live on after this life ends.

Chapter Five

Reincarnation

What the Buddha said of death.
Life is a journey.
Death is a return to earth.
The universe is like an inn.
The passing years are like dust.

Regard this phantom world
As a star at dawn, a bubble in a stream,
A flash of lightning in a summer cloud,
A flickering lamp, a phantom, and a dream.

The two religions most people associate with the concept of reincarnation are Buddhism and Hinduism. Each have a different definition of what reincarnation is.

Buddhism was based on the teachings of Siddartha Guatama, who is known as the Buddha, which means "the awakened one." The Buddha is said to have lived on the eastern part of the sub continent of India during the 6th and 4th century B.C. Buddhism is practiced for the most part in Asia, but is found on other parts of the globe as well.

In the Buddhist religion, it is taught that each cycle of death and rebirth is to be avoided by obtaining the ultimate spiritual state of Nirvana. Nirvana is reached by the releasing of one's personal identity and desires. To enter the state of Nirvana the individual's personality and experiences must dissolve or dismantle and cease to exist. What remains is a stream of consciousness that becomes Buddha, only Buddhas can enter Nirvana.

Buddhists believe that there is no permanent essence that exists after the death of the physical body, but elements of individual identity that make up the individual. These elements are emotions, physical phenomena, sensory perceptions, and consciousness. These elements are what survives the death of the physical body, but do not take the form of an immortal soul. There are two major Buddhist schools of thought.

They are Theravada (South East Asia) and Mahayana (India, China, Japan). In the Pali tradition which belongs to the Theravada school of thought, it is taught that Karma(the law of cause and effect by which each individual creates their own destiny by his or her thoughts, words, and deeds). and nothing from your previous life will continue to exist in reincarnation. Reincarnation is one life ending and another beginning with similar Karma. Reincarnation happens instantly upon death of the physical body, and a new life is started.

In the Mahayana school, there is an after life or in between place to go before rebirth, known as pure land. Pure land is a place free of sadness, want, and fear. The purpose of pure land is to give the deceased rebirth into a life where it will be easier for that incarnation to achieve Nirvana.

Hinduism, believed to be the world's oldest religion, also teaches reincarnation. Hinduism precedes recorded history, and has no human founder. It's origins began in India between 4,000 and 10,000 B.C. As with Buddhism,

Hinduism also teaches the law of Karma. Hindus believe that the soul reincarnates evolving through several cycles of death and rebirth until all bad Karma has been resolved. When freedom from this cycle is reached, the soul reaches Moksha, and is no longer reincarnated. Hinduism is a polytheistic religion with many deities. There are female goddesses (devas) and male gods. With the supreme deities being, Shiva Vishnu and Shakti. Unlike Buddhism, Hindus believe that a soul will sometimes reincarnate in animal form in order to work out very bad Karma.

Hindus also teach that no one religion is the only way for a soul to attain salvation, but that all genuine paths are pathways to Gods light deserving of tolerance and understanding.

My knowledge of reincarnation has come from my memories of my past incarnations, as well as what I have received intuitively from the spirit world. Our souls will experience several incarnations on this planet until we have learned whatever lesson(s) our soul needs to experience. What we don't master in one lifetime, we will continue within the next life until we have learned what we need for soul growth. We don't choose what we need to learn, but we do choose how we learn these lessons before we return to earth. Every soul learns the same lessons, but not always in the same way, or order. For example a soul can choose to put off a difficult lesson, or learn it in stages, some of us will choose to learn a lesson with one single life changing event, others might choose to learn that same lesson in multiple lives, or as a theme in one life. For example if learning to deal with rejection is the lesson, one might have issues with holding on to a relationship. The outcome is the same, but the speed in which the soul advances is different. The life your living now along with you previous incarnation(s) is in reality one life, interrupted by your soul switching bodies in order to learn or continue to learn your lessons. All of these life experiences adds to you personality on the other side, only the positive aspects of your soul remain on the other side. Before we are born we decide with our guides how we are going to tackle each lesson. We choose in advance which souls we will reincarnate with, and they are all factors in how we chart our lives. Our guides, God, and our loved ones we are returning to earth with, will not let us choose anything that we can not handle on a soul level.

Reincarnation adds a sense of fairness to life and spirituality. If we are to believe we only live one life on this planet, then we would need to come to the conclusion that the powers that be are so completely unfair that they randomly decide who will be born rich, sick, poor, etc. Making these choices without any real justification other than they felt like it. Or you could believe innocent people are punished for the bad deeds of those who came before them. Spirit is not that cruel. Reincarnation is more logical and carries with it justice, fairness, and a sense of order. There is an actual reason, even if we do not actively remember at this moment, why one soul may breeze through life, while another is in a constant state of struggle. It supports the belief that absolutely everything happens for a distinct reason.

Not everyone can remember their past lives. If you had all of your memories or even a few extra bouncing around in your memory, it would be very easily to become distracted with the memories of the past. The focus needs to remain on the here and now. This life right at this moment needs to remain your souls focus. We remember on a soul level. When we meet those we knew in previous incarnations, we recognize them right away. We all have had that don't I know you from somewhere moment and we search our memory banks for where we know the person we just meant from. Now imagine if your past live memories came up suddenly at that moment you would spend time reminiscing with the soul you just were reunited with instead of focusing on this life's lesson. For those of us that can recall our past incarnations, it is because that past life's theme is still playing itself out now in your current situation. You are still learning those very same lessons. Examine which kinds of situations seem to keep happening and repeating in your life. The good situations and the bad. Those are the parts of your life that need attention. The bad need to be worked on to the best of your ability. Sometimes just becoming aware of them is enough to make the changes you need. The good situations that keep repeating are happening so that you can learn to be appreciative and grateful.

Our souls are in a constant state of learning while we are experiencing life on the earth plane. Every journey we choose to experience here on earth has meaning. We are all connected we all have meaning every journey has value no matter how complicated, short, or simple a journey maybe, they are all equal in the eyes of spirit.

There are times during readings I can peer into the past life of a client. When that client has an unresolved past life issue I will see them briefly dressed in the clothing of that time period. I then will see scenes in my mind's eye from that past life that tell the tale of that life. I then tell the client about the issue that needs to be addressed.

Each one of us does remember their past lives on a soul level. The periods in history that you have always felt drawn to or have been fascinated with, is where your past lives were experienced. Your soul will be drawn to places, cultures, time periods you experienced. Your favorite hobbies ans activities are also clues to where you lived, and what your occupation was. Dreams of faraway lands and people you only recognize while dreaming of them also tell the tale of our past.

Past life regression, where you are hypnotized and brought back to a time before you were born, is another tool that can help you piece together the puzzle of your past.

I have active memories of several of my previous incarnations. They are memories like any other that I have had since childhood. When I was a child I would reminisce about these places I hadn't been in this lifetime. It wasn't until I was older I realized these memories happened before I was living in this body.

I have clear memories of ancient Egypt. I was a man of some influence. I recall walking through Karnac and gazing at the architecture, and admiring the statues. When

I was a teenager I had a detailed dream about the Sphinx. In the dream I was shown that the Sphinx had a tunnel leading to a chamber underneath of it. With the opening being at the front of the right paw. As I am writing this I am being shown that the chamber contains pieces of Rosetta type stones, keys to translating lost languages, scrolls with detailed information on how exactly the pyramids were constructed, and the secrets to the origins of man. There is also a body or mummy of a Pharaoh located in the center of the chamber.

Later I learned of similar theories that have been brought forth by archaeologists.

The next life I recall I was a male living in ancient Rome. What happens to me in this life I have not found any historical records of. I'm tied to a stake that has been placed in the middle of the coliseum. It is a brutally hot day and I'm sweating under the hot sun. I'm not sure how it is placed on me but I am covered in a substance that looks like honey. I can't see what direction they come from, but suddenly a swarm of bees covers me and I am stung repeatedly by angry bees.

My next incarnation memory is of a life experienced in 1500's England. I recall belonging to a group of women. We are all surrounding a woman I believe to be royalty, we are all assisting her as she is getting dressed. I can remember the way the sunlight came through the window and hit the thin piece of cloth I was holding making it appear to be a beautiful shade of peachy pink. My next recollection is not as bright. I am locked in a prison. The walls are gray and made of stone. The door that holds me in is black and made of iron. It's cold and dark and wet. I have one arm chained to the prison wall, the other is left free. Next thing that happens, a man with a black hood comes to remove me from the cell. Next I am on the top of a castle tower. Its nighttime and the moon is full. I notice the light from the full moon shining beautifully off of the water below. Then, I place my head on the wood block.

It wasn't until I was older, I saw photos of the tower of London and chills went through me as I instantly knew I had been there. I did some limited research on women who were executed at the tower. I couldn't find any one who fit with my memories. But we have to remember back in that time, a lot happened that simply didn't get recorded. History was at the mercy of whoever was in control. Also records could have easily been destroyed or lost.

Another past life I have fond recollections of is living as a Native American male, living in the Black Hills area of the United States. In this life I fought against the U.S. cavalry. I can recall my horse which was a light beige color with a dark black mane. I painted him with signs and symbols to protect us both, make us invisible during battle. It was a sunny cloudless day, I was riding looking for cavalry soldiers. We were not engaged in an active battle at that moment, but I was looking to see who was encroaching on our village. I was riding my horse up an embankment. A cavalry member who was riding alone, crossed my path. As soon as he saw us he took off on his horse, and I began chasing him. When I was close enough. I whacked him in the head with my club as hard as I could. I laughed as his hat flew off with the blow and he fell off of his horse. My next memory of this life, I am standing on the edge of a cliff, and gazing down at beautiful scenery that resembles the grand canyon, on yet another warm clear sunny day. I stand there for a moment then proceed to throw myself off.

My love for this culture did not die with me on that day. It is very much alive with me still to this day. So much so that I still consider those I lived that life with my true ancestors I feel them with me each and every day. I have unfinished business with that life I feel because quite frankly, my people from that life not only lost the battle, they were all but annihilated from history. I consider what happened a holocaust of a supreme culture of people. My blood still boils today when I think about what happened. I'm not sure I want to solve my unresolved issues from that life, a part of me is afraid I will lose my passion for the culture and people I miss so dearly.

Something I feel I should add here. When I was younger I recall my father telling us, my brothers and I, that we were of Navajo descent. I was really intrigued by this due to my love of Native culture and of course my dreams. Sometime later I was thinking about what he had said and decided to approach him and find out more about my heritage. So I did and he proceeded to deny he had ever said such a thing and ended our conversation. So needless to say, I had a row of question marks over my head. I decided to ask both of my older brother separately about what my father had said and they both confirmed that my father had in fact told us that we have Navajo heritage. I was happy to find out I wasn't remembering incorrectly but still had and have questions about what he told us.

My validation that these events actually happened to me, my soul is the strength of the emotions I feel when I recall these events. The fact that there is absolutely no way that as as a child I could have not only known what these places looked liked, but also the historical elements attached to them is further evidence that the soul experiences more than one incarnation on this planet.

I cherish my past life memories. They have shown me the evidence I need that our bodies do in fact contain a soul. Having these memories then later seeing the photos of these places, has been an amazing part of my spiritual journey. I have taken pieces of these lives and incorporated them into my present, in the form of my religious beliefs. I don't fall into any particular religious box. I always say I believe in God not labels. I have a great respect for the Egyptian Gods, Native American believes and practices, bits and pieces of Christian teachings, with some ancient Celtic and Pagan beliefs of Europe thrown into the mix. All of my past life experiences, have added to the mosaic of my soul.

Chapter Six

The Archangels and Mary Magdalene

Angels were created by God(s.) to be our protectors, healers, and message bringers. During meditations I am able to channel some of those messages. I will be sharing messages from Archangel Michael, Raphael, Gabriel, Uriel, Raguel, and Chamuel. I also included prayers to help you connect with these Angels when you feel the need. There is never a wrong time to ask for assistance. If you feel the need in your heart and soul, for Angel guidance, that is all you need to call on them for help, guidance, and protection.

Archangel Michael (who is like God), was the first Angel created by God. He was created to be in charge of truth, courage, and integrity. He was created to protect mankind in every way, emotionally, physically, and psychically. He is the Archangel that is the leader of the army of God that fights against evil. In the new testament it is said "there was a war in heaven. Michael and his Angels fought against the dragon, and the dragon and his Angels fought back. But he was not strong enough and they lost their place in heaven."

In Jewish tradition, Michael acted as the advocate of Israel and sometimes fought with the princes of the other nations, and Samael, Israel's adversary. It is said when Samael was thrown from heaven he tried to take hold of Michael's wings, whom he wanted to bring down with him as he fell from heaven. But Michael was saved by God.

Archangel Michael protects the souls of light that work here on the earth plane. The light bringers who are working on earth to remove it from its negative state.

Michael's message, I protect souls from the negative energies that scare us, or aim to make us depressed, give up our mission. Archangels are extensions of the God energy male and female. There is God who is an equal balance of masculine and feminine, then Archangels, souls of man, animals, plants, earth and it's elements. That is the natural order. There are no demons. There are souls of animals and man that are negative and dark. There has to be at least on the earth plane, a balance of positive and negative energies or souls. The earth plane is out of balance and the negative energies are "taking over." The more souls that aware of this, the better the chance that we can get the earth back on track. The earth plane will always have negative energies existing on it. They are here to teach and help the positive energies, to grow and learn. I protect the light workers while they are bringing the earth plane back into balance.

Archangel Michael is an angel that I call on quite often. The negative energies that are around, tend to be drawn to sensitive people like myself because they know not only do we notice them, we are easy targets to drain energy from. The astral nasties as I call them also enjoy hanging around mediums like myself in an attempt to scare them away from spirit communication. The last thing negative energies want is someone like myself delivering healing messages from the other side to people here on the earth plane. They will try to distract me and people like myself from their life's mission, especially in our early years, before we realize what is happening. Archangel Michael will come through for you, protect you, and show you the way. When I notice their presence, which at my age now it is more of an annoyance, then fearful experience, putting me in a snippy mood, or making the room ice cold, I start my sage burning ritual an call on Archangel Michael. I visualize Archangel Michael cutting the negative energy away from me and sometimes, impaling the negative energy and flinging it away from me.

Archangel Michael is also a protector for law enforcement, fire fighters, paramedics and military personnel. Protecting those who put their lives on the line everyday to protect and save citizens. I'm including three different prayers to help you connect with Archangel Michael. The first is the short catholic prayer, then the prayer I composed for personal use, and one I composed for law enforcement, firefighters, paramedics, and military personnel.

Short Prayer to St. Michael the Archangel

Saint Michael the Archangel, defend us in battle, be our protection against the malice and snares of the devil. May God rebuke him we humbly pray; and do thou, O prince of the Heavenly host, by the power of God, thrust into hell Satan and all evil spirits who wander through the world for the ruin of souls. Amen.

My personal prayer is simple and easy to remember. When I use it I visualize Archangel Michael cutting at the negative energy and removing it with his sword. I also envision my surroundings filled with white light, to empty my space of any and all darkness.

Archangel Michael, brave and strong, protect me from the negative energies who wish to disrupt my work, discourage me from communicating with souls of light, by filling me with fear of the unknown. Take your sword and cut the negative energies to pieces, take your sword, impale the negative energies and fling them back from where they came. Amen.

My prayer for law enforcement, fire fighters, paramedics, and military personnel. I composed a special one for those who work in these fields because their work can be extremely emotionally draining. The negative energies that are around would like nothing more than to have those who save lives on a regular basis, or catch the bad guys, dwell on the times the bad guy got away or someone just could not be saved. Archangel Michael will give you the strength to keep fighting and remind you of all the people that were saved because you did your job successfully.

Archangel Michael, my protector, my guardian, my defender through the fight. Protect me from harm and keep my focus on justice, to keep fighting for what is right, to remove evil from the streets of this world, and lock it away where it can harm no more. Help me protect the innocent, the defenseless, the weak. Give me the strength to walk through the fire, the accident scene, the land mines and bullets, to protect and save the injured. Amen.

Archangel Michael, as well as the others are available to all of us in our time of need. All of the Archangels can be in more than one place at a time just as God can be. The difference being, God stays put on the Other Side, and the Archangels can help from the Other Side, or here on the earth plane. And at times masquerading as one of us.

Archangel Raphael

The next Archangel, Raphael is said to be the fourth Archangel created by God. His name means "God heals" and it is said he healed the earth when it was defiled by the sins of the fallen Angels. He is the patron of the blind, happy meetings, nurses, doctors, match makers, and travelers.

His message for those who heal the sick, I will give you the strength to keep working to heal others after you have lost a patient or feel as if there is no hope for an individual. I will remind you why you chose the healing profession, and at times help you to connect the dots with what seems like an impossible patient.

Archangel Raphael's message for the sick and suffering. Call one me for the strength to keep fighting and to remind me of why you are fighting to get better. Those miracle cures, think of me ask and I am there. When you can not find the answer to your health issue, I will guide you to the Doctor who is right for you. Call on me to ease your pain I will give you the strength to keep fighting. When you are praying for yourself or a sick loved one including your beloved animals, envision me there with you wrapping my wings around you, or your loved one as you bask in my beautiful healing green light.

For coma patients, their families must call on myself and Archangel Michael to watch over them. Myself for healing, Archangel Michael for protection against negative energies, for coma opens a portal to the Other Side.

Prayer to help you connect with Archangel Raphael, Wrap your healing wings around me. Take my pain and remove it from me. Give me the strength to keep fighting. Deliver to my doctor(s) what they need to heal me. Lead my doctor(s) to the fountain of healing knowledge. Amen.

Prayer for the healing of a sick loved one,

Archangel Raphael, please come and wrap your healing wings around my loved one. Take their pain and carry it away. Take their fears and wash them away. Give them the strength they need to keep fighting. Amen.

Archangel Gabriel

Archangel Gabriel's message contained some information I did not expect. It did answer some personal questions of mine, I hope it will for you as well. Gabriel name translates to God is my strength. Gabriel is the ultimate messenger. The Archangel sent by God to tell Mary she was going to be the Mother of the son of God. And his job remains just that, to continue to bring messages to God's children. Gabriel sends messages to people through dreams and premonitions. Archangel Gabriel delivered the message and the way to connect all within the same message, I was having trouble keeping up and at times started writing letters I had never seen. So, I will type the message just as it was given, maybe change the order of a sentence or two, but it will remain the same message. As you read, you should be able to tell the difference between the way to connect and the message.

Archangel Gabriel's message,

Turn to me when you need help for your future, look to the sky out on a starry spring night, gaze at the little dipper laying on the grass. Before you fall asleep envision me there with you, above you in the starry sky. And I will appear to you in your dream and show you a vision of your future. A loving mission filled with grace you will do unto others with love and patience. Look to the starry sky, the little dipper. Gaze at the center your dream may have the stars move and form letters that become words to answer your question, bring your message. I am the stars, the sky, home is the universe the stars above the Angels, God is the sun. Love is the energy, gravity, orbits, movement that keeps it going. Planets are different levels of home. Man is alien to earth some not all. Some that are native to earth have no soul only darkness the light was brought here. Remember who you are. My message to humans listen to light workers we guide them, they guide you to a better earth. The North Star is the center of the universe the all. Black holes are tunnels- portals to different dimensions. Fear not the darkness- they are illusion only real is the light -love all that matter- the all. Knowing being penetrates everything.

I am the only Archangel who can appear as both male and female. The other Archangels have two separate forms one male one female. I appear to you as the one you are most comfortable with.

Archangel Uriel

Uriel translates to "Light of God" or "God is My Light" the Archangel of wisdom. He sometimes appears as a cherub. He shines the light of God's truth into the darkness of confusion. Archangel Uriel is there to help with learning, decision making, solve problems, new creative ideas, and resolve conflicts.

Archangel Uriel's message,

Call on me when you need help with life's difficult decisions, which school to attend, what your major should be. Connect with me by using automatic writing. For those who have never tried just concentrate on my energy simply by lighting a red candle and a second white candle. And just start writing anything and everything that comes to mind even if it seems outrageous. Stop when you feel comfortable, but you should try and keep writing for about two minutes. Go through what you have written re-write anything that seems disorganized. And sort through all of it. The answer will come. For those already studying, carry a representation of me with you during difficult exams, I will help you concentrate on the correct answers. I help with the light bulb moments in scientific discoveries, and difficult mathematical formulas. I will also nudge you to stay away from dangerous situations listen to your intuition when you feel it.

Prayer to help you connect with Archangel Uriel,

Archangel Uriel, guide me to the place of knowledge, the place of wisdom, to enable me to make the appropriate choice for my life's plan. And to inspire my creative ideas, my intellectual endeavors. Amen.

Archangel Raguel

Archangel Raguel's name is translated, "friend of God." He is the Archangel of justice and harmony. His job is to work for Gods will to be done among his fellow Angels. Supervising and overseeing the work of the other angels. He watches over the work assignments that God has given the other angels and holds them accountable. Call on Archangel Raguel to overcome mistreatment and get the respect you deserve. Archangel Raguel is also there to help resolve conflicts, bring order to chaos, and aid those in need to stay true to their spiritual convictions under pressure.

Archangel Raguel's message,

Children of God, call to me when justice is needed. When there is conflict between good friends and family I will give you the answers to resolve your problems.

Detectives, Lawyers, Judges, ask of me for help with your toughest cases and it is done.

If a criminal walks free they will live a life of misery. No one escapes justice, if not in this life, than the next. Those who use the justice system to knowingly aid a criminal will suffer punishment as well. I record and watch it all, God punishes.

Prayer to connect with Archangel Raguel,

Archangel Raguel, I ask you to help me find the right answers, the right words, to solve my conflict with my dear friend, my family. Show me the way to peaceful words, a peaceful solution. Amen.

For the wrong fully accused, Archangel Raguel, protect my innocence, show me lead me to a lawyer who can defend/ prosecute my case properly. Give the judge clear, fair vision of my case. Amen.

For judges, lawyers, and detectives,

Archangel Raguel,

Lead me to the evidence I need to make my case, make the proper ruling, catch the appropriate criminal. Amen.

Archangel Chamuel

Archangel Chamuel "He who sees God." The Archangel of love. Archangel Chamuel is there for those who desire to strengthen a loving bond. A parent child bond, or if you need help feeling love for yourself, Archangel Chamuel is there. If you are lonely and broken hearted, or desire to feel more connected to God's love, Archangel Chamuel will be there for you.

Archangel Chamuel's message,

Seek my love when a relationship needs healing, when you feel there is no love left in your heart call on me. When you feel the need to forgive those you love, I will show you how. When you are questioning Gods love in your life, call on me I will show you the way to God's grace, understanding, acceptance, and love.

Prayer to connect with Archangel Chamuel,

Archangel Chamuel, I ask you, to show me the way to love, understanding, forgiveness. Show me how to love those close to me I have conflicts with. Show me Gods love help me to feel the presence of God in my life. Amen.

The following chart is a list of candle colors to use while connecting with the Archangels.

Archangel Michael: Blue and White
Archangel Raphael: Green and White
Archangel Gabriel: Pink and White
Archangel Uriel: Red and White
Archangel Raguel: Silver or Copper and White
Archangel Chamuel: Pink and White

Archangel messages are open for all who are willing to listen. Let go of what you expect or want to hear, and be open to any and all information. Begin by sitting in a quiet place. Light the appropriate candles, place your personal representation of the Archangel you wish to connect with near you. Relax, take your time taking deep cleansing breaths, relaxing each muscle of your body as you exhale. Take your time breathing deeply as many times as you feel you need to. Keep your eyes closed and visualize yourself with your Archangel in a favorite place, imagined or an actual place you enjoy being. Say the prayer given in this chapter, or say your own, and listen. Listen with your heart and mind pay attention to your emotions and how you are feeling. When you are ready open your eyes. Keep a journal nearby and right away write down everything you felt, saw, and heard. Read through what you wrote, your answers will come to you.

Mary Magdalene

My reason for deciding to try and connect with Mary Magdalene began one afternoon a few months back. We were driving back home after shopping and I had one of my light bulb moments, where information from my guide will "pop" into my mind. These moments always stand out and get my attention because it will be information I never thought of, about a subject that is far from my mind at that particular moment. So we are heading down a scenic Virginia country road, not talking about much, and I'm listening to our favorite rock station, and watching the cows and horses munching on grass as we go whizzing by. When from "nowhere" the phrase "Jesus and Mary Magdalene were brother and sister." Came to me. Well, I was shocked. But at the same time it explained why they were never intimate with each other despite how close they were. She also seemed to be from what I have read and heard over the years one of his favorite people. So it was from here that I really wanted to find out more. The following is the information I received when I connected with her. Mary Magdalene's message,

I was the younger sister of Jesus. There were three sons and one daughter, Jesus was the youngest of the sons. Then I was born and named after my mother Mary. Jesus and I are soul mates. Soul mates can be of any strong bond not solely romantic or a lover relationship. We are light workers who work as a team. We always return (incarnate) together, no exceptions. Our childhood was beautiful with loving parents, we were well educated and a religious family. I looked up to all of my brothers but Jesus and I were inseparable. He protected me and loved me. I had a prophetic dream when I was very young of his crucifixion It haunted me every day. I told him of it, but he wanted us to go forth and teach. He said if that is my fate, then so be it. It was as if a part of him knew this would happen as well and he was at peace with it. A lot of Jesus' life was left out of historic record, and simply lost, and not recorded over his years. Because of the time gap, and many translations over many years, a lot was left out, some intentionally. Whoever was the translating party, edited information to fit their own selfish needs. What was left out about my role as an influential woman, was done to promote Christianity as a patriarchal religion. Women could not be seen as equals to the political structure of that time. When I say of that time, the time of the first translations, and recordings of the new testament. The old testament was altered as well. I was to be seen as Jesus' equal, Mother of all life, love, bringer of beauty and peace, I gave prophecies and healed the sick as Jesus did, beside him until the end. We wanted future religions to mirror us in churches, places of worship, a male and female Rabbi, a Priest and Priestess, not the male dominated religions that followed. My story was twisted beyond recognition, distorted, and made perverted. I suffered a similar fate. After the crucifixion of my dear brother, I was cast into the dessert where I suffered until I finally succumbed from starvation. There are records of Jesus and our travels and teachings that were not destroyed that will bring my story to light and I will be honored as intended. They lie underground at a place built upon, a modern day home, in Iran. Maybe another century they will be found by accident by a small girl, playing. I will keep visiting the children, healing their pain, drying their tears, I am their protector, their healing love.

If you are able to see me as Jesus' equal, his counterpart, you will be honoring my work, and lifting all women to the spiritual level that was always intended.

My thoughts, the message I received from Mary Magdalene I feel came at this point in our history because I feel the majority of the world can handle it. It is time for women to stand up and take a more active role in their faith. Women as well as men will benefit greatly from elevating women to the spiritual role they were always meant to have. When that happens, women's rights will progress even further, and sexism will become a thing of the past.

Chapter Seven

Messages From Home

What is it like to crossover to the other side? What is life like for our loved ones who have made the journey back home? The answer is buried deep inside all of our sub conscious minds. That is where mediums like myself come in. It is part of our life's journey to remember for those of you that can't. It is simply not part of your life's plan. If everyone was meant to recall home we would. But for most of us it would get in the way and we would not care or forget what we are here for. We all need to focus on our individual life chart and full fill our goals. We can all benefit from a reminder, a message to give us validation that there is purpose for everyone's life. And that this life here on earth has meaning, and a lesson for us all.

I will begin with what it is like to crossover. When we first leave our bodies, we will be greeted by our guides, who we will instantly recognize, and a loved one who has passed before us. A loved one can be a family member, a close friend, even a beloved pet. A lot of my readings have shown this. Spirit will come through to say they knew they had crossed when they were met by their favorite childhood pet. Your loved one and spirit guide will travel with you over the veil to the other side. Some souls will use a tunnel, some a staircase to the other side. Some will just instantly be there. You will feel no fear only peace love and acceptance. The first place most often seen, from what I have been told, is a beautiful field of colorful flowers that pop up through long strands of yellow grass. Something like a scene from a beautiful Midwest summer. With a majestic blue mountain in view but off in the distance. Your guide and others, there is no limit to how many of your loved ones show up to support you, will walk you through this glorious field to a building. This building resembles an ancient Greek temple without windows or walls just beautiful gleaming white columns holding the structure together. This building is called the Hall of Review. Here you will meet with Archangel Jeremiel to review your life. You will feel the emotions of how you made others feel, and come to an understanding of how your actions affected others for good and for bad. You will "walk a mile in their shoes." And analyze what went wrong and what went right so that a comparison can be mad with the chart you created before birth. There is actually no wrong or right it is all in the lessons that fit into the bigger picture or purpose of your individual chart. You must sort through it all to find if there are any unfinished lessons, or unfinished business between your soul and another soul. You must establish if you accomplished your life's goals to the best of your ability. It is at this time you will decide if you want to reincarnate or not. If you do chose to come back and live on earth again, you do not need to come back right away. But when the decision to return is made, you have to full fill your choice. It is not a choice taken lightly. The earth plane is for the bravest of souls. When you have made the decision to reincarnate, your soul prepares by reviewing the incomplete lessons of your previous incarnations.

You may have unfinished business from more than one incarnation. We almost always incarnate with the same souls especially if we need to finish what we started so there may already be such a soul on the other side that passed before you, or you may have to wait for a soul to join you and then wait for that soul to decide whether or not they want to incarnate again. There is a lot of planning that takes place before we reincarnate. First the decision to comeback, Second which lesson we want to finish, and third which souls are willing to make the trip back with us in order to help us, as well as work on their own lessons. There can be exceptions made and new souls introduced to you if the souls you are already familiar with don't want to reincarnate when you feel you want to. Once we get the first stages in planning done, we start writing our charts, and decide how we want to learn our lessons. We compare with other souls until we come to our agreement. Along with our lessons and unfinished business, at this time we choose our parents, friends, adversaries, pets, careers, talents, religious beliefs, and medical issues. We choose it all before we return. It is all part of our life's plan.

If you find you have unfinished business, but want to stay home, you can handle your lessons by doing good for other souls on the other side. You can train to become a spirit guide. Spirit guides, as they guide others, are also learning lessons and evolving spiritually while helping other souls through life. Spirit guides train by learning all about the soul they will be guiding, all of their past lives, professions, and relationship issues. By becoming a spirit guide, one of the biggest lessons is how to give of yourself in the most unselfish of ways, for when you are a spirit guide, it is all about the soul you are guiding and how you are learning from them. Spirit guides will use what they are learning as a guide, to not only grow spiritually themselves, but in the training of future guides as well. Archangels and guides will take what they have observed and use it for every soul on the other side, not just guides in training. There is no limit except the end of soul growth, to how many times a soul can become a guide. A spirit guide can exist here on the physical plane, and on the other side simultaneously.

As soon as you make the decision to become a guide the training begins. You will be taken by your guide who hasn't left your side quite yet, to another building called the hall of learning. Here you will first spend time with your guide and he/she will explain how they helped you during your time on earth, and what you taught them. Then you will join other souls in training and your guide will no longer be your guide, and your training will begin. Your training will be given by former guides and overseen by the Archangels both male and female that exist on the other side. As soon as you complete your training you will meet with the soul who is getting ready to reincarnate and spend time going over their chart and life plan. Every soul's chart is kept in a library on the other side. When we are in our physical bodies we experience Déjà- vu. That is our soul remembering what we charted for ourselves, and validation we are on the right path.

How do our loved ones send us signs from the other side? When our soul is living on the other side, we are existing at a higher vibration. It is very difficult for souls to show themselves in such a way that they can be photographed or seen by the naked eye. Every now and then it happens and some of us are lucky enough to see a spirit and have this experience. Because it is so difficult for spirit to show themselves, spirit will use our physical world and the objects and animals around us to make their presence known. One of the easiest energies for spirit to manipulate is electricity. Spirit will flick lights, shut appliances off, freeze computers, ring the phone, and cause radio interference. Spirit will use animals as well. Butterflies are commonly used by spirit to send signs. Sometimes spirit will take on the form of a bird, insect or animal to get your attention. Other common signs are knocking, dreams, smells, light physical touches, and songs. How does spirit know when to send these signs? Spirit is always aware of when we are thinking of them. Will it happen every time we are thinking of them? No. But be patient and pay attention to the subtle signs and you will notice. Let go of what you expect or want for a sign, and pay attention to the ways in which spirit is able to communicate with you. Remind yourself of their favorite flowers, pets, songs, perfumes. And keep a dream journal. Pay extra attention on anniversaries, holidays, family gatherings, and birthdays. Special events like a new baby joining the family are also an active time for spirit around you.

How can I send messages to spirit?

You are sitting alone an your loved one who has passed crosses through your memory banks. This is the perfect time to grab a pen and paper and write down everything you are thinking and feeling at that moment. They know how you are feeling and what you are writing. Go ahead and write them a letter. Read it out loud. Don't be afraid to speak to them, they can hear and see us even if we can't hear and see them. Talking to a favorite picture is also an excellent way to connect and may feel a little more comfortable than speaking into the air. Also holding an article of clothing, a piece of jewelry, a book or favorite belonging, may help bring the spiritual energy closer. Something we all should remember they can see, hear, and feel our emotions. Come out of that place that tells us, that because we can no longer see our loved ones who have passed, they must truly be gone, and know deep inside your heart that is not true.

It is easier for us to communicate with spirit then for spirit to communicate with us. They appreciate being acknowledged here on the physical plane, and it can be healing for us as well.

The journey back home to the other side is not to be feared. You are loved and protected by your guides, angels, and loved ones throughout the entire process. No one dies alone.

The following are posts from my blog Messages From Home. I receive these messages during automatic writing sessions. I'm including these messages to show some additional examples of signs our loved ones send to all of us from home.

Searching For Answers

July 25, 2014

Today's message is from a Mother to her son. She shows me piles and piles of books. Books on the table, bookshelves reaching to the ceiling stuffed full of books. Not sure if it was her or her son who had the book obsession possibly both, but books were the obsession for the household. The subject matter was less important than the fact it was printed on paper and held together between a cover. She shows me that she is the one who gave her son his first book on science which soon became a lifelong obsession as well. She was strict, don't ask questions just do what I say, all business, very serious, and at times overbearing. She said she acted this way out of love. She wanted her son to reach his full potential. She bragged about her sons academic achievements every chance she could, and was very, very proud. She shows me a scrapbook she kept which contained a newspaper article. She says "You were my world the center of my universe." Wanted so much for her son to have an easier life, and not have to struggle like she did. Visiting the west coast was the last time they saw each other. She says her son still looks at the photos taken there and wonders why she didn't tell him how sick she really was. "I couldn't bear to say those words to my son." "I didn't suffer I was here then I was gone quick as that." She says "People in your life care more about you than you realize don't be afraid to open up to people." She then shows me collections of items her son kept from the 80's and teenage years. Then, journals packed full of religious material. Any and every religion ever worshiped on this planet, researched, compared, examined and researched for years. Looking for answers about life and death, as well as a new way of thinking, reconciling the divine truths with the scientific. She says "Look no further than your own heart." " I send signs in the form of dreams." "Those visitations are real please know this." She also knocks objects off shelves, and pictures from the wall. She ends with "I'll be around." "Love from Mom."

Bluebird

June 23, 2014

This message is from a daughter to her parents. Once again, I'm sharing so that everyone who reads can gain something from the message. She starts by showing me her Mother tearfully removing cards from the hospital wall in her room. She still has these cards tucked away at home. She then makes reference to the hospital food, She says" They didn't have my favorite breakfast food so someone would bring it in for her." She jokes about laying in bed all day. "There is only so much television one can watch." If someone would punch a hole in the ceiling I could at least gaze at the stars while I'm lying here." She then shows me a collection of scarves. "Good thing I kept them." She says. She tells me she has no regrets an led a happy full life. "I saw places and had experiences others only dream of." She kept a detailed journal of her illness, in hopes it would eventually reach others and help them through their difficult times. She showed me pillows and blankets that were brought in from home, her favorite had a small bird embroidered on the front. She then shows me a scene from childhood where she keeps taking off her Mother's glasses and trying to wear them. Her Mom read from the Bible at her bedside (a favorite passage.) she says "Thank you, I heard every word." She leaves signs in the form of little trinkets her Mother and niece find scattered about. Another sign involves a wall photo that is constantly being straightened, then "moved." "That's me she says. " I move the photo!" "Thank you for honoring me, my life." She then shows me stacks of writings around the house. "You should really get organized mum." She then makes a reference to Jazz music and the song "I'll be seeing you." Her Father dreamed of her, and saw her in the bedroom. Shows me Bluebirds. She stretches out her arms, opens her hands, and Bluebird flies out and into the sky above. "We all go home when it's our time never too soon."

Chapter Eight

Anatomy of a Reading

In this chapter I am going to break down a reading from beginning to end to draw a picture of how a reading works from the perspective of the medium. I will begin with a brief explanation of how a reading begins, with examples of how spirit uses my senses to get the message through. Then I will breakdown a reading into individual parts.

First, I give four different types of readings. Phone, e-mail, in person, and on-line. Aside from the on-line readings, each type requires the client to first make an appointment. I know nothing about the person except their first name and phone number. Every reading begins with an explanation of how I receive information from the spirit world.

"Before I begin, I ask my guide and angels to bring me the information that will be of the most healing for you at this time in your life." "I ask to connect with your passed loved ones who can send you the love and healing you need right now in your life." I then explain that you might not connect with the soul you are hoping to. Not because they do not want to communicate, but spirit feels another message will be better for you right now." Spirit sends the messages that you need, not necessarily what you want.

As I begin to connect, spirit will start to show me mental images of the message they are trying to communicate. Along with the mental images, I will feel the emotions that are coming through as well. I the will put those emotions into words. For example I might say, "She is saying you feel sorry you didn't get the chance to say goodbye before she passed." I'm not hearing the voice of spirit say those words, I'm feeling the emotion and then putting that emotion into words for the client. When I feel the emotion, it is as if it is happening to me and I am experiencing the emotional pain, or loving feelings first hand. It can be very easy to misinterpret a message. One instance this happened during a reading a woman showed me the inside of a classroom with school age children. I felt as if this was a happy period in her life. I thought the image meant she had been a teacher, but it turned out she hadn't gone that far in her education. A reminder to myself to slow down and take my time with the meaning behind the message. I feel like the feeling of loss maybe what I missed in this example. In that instance spirit was sending the absolute correct message, it was my interpretation that was wrong.

Along with mental images and emotions I will receive bodily sensations, tastes and smells. Often the bodily sensations will tell the tale of how the person passed on, and sometimes a health condition they suffered from during life.

I was connecting with the spirit of a woman when suddenly my left side felt numb. It turned out the woman had passed of a stroke. At times these sensations can be unnerving for me, but it only lasts for a moment and I know spirit is only doing this to help me get the proper message through. Other examples are coughing or feeling as if I can't breathe, feeling pressure in certain areas of my body, or tightness around my throat. I have never felt actual physical pain just pressure or a quick numbness. Often when a spirit comes through who has passed of cancer I will get a bitter taste in my mouth and a nauseous feeling. I feel a similar sensation when one has passed from an overdose.

Hearing spirit is not my strongest psychic sense. When I do hear it, it is barely audible and very hard to hear exactly what is being said. I will sometimes hear a noise associated with how someone passed, cars on dirt roads, or sometimes a song will come through.

Smells that spirit will use to bring messages are almost always favorite foods, smoke, and perfumes. Spirit uses my senses to the best of its ability to get the proper message through.

I will be using a reading I gave on-line for this example. The woman I read for posted a photo of her mother in-law who had recently passed. When I give a reading via photo I get the information in the same manner as every other type of reading. First spirit will give me a few specific details to help me validate that I am in fact connecting with spirit, and not just picking up on photo cues. I will be repeating the reading just as it was given on the photo, with explanations added where I believe they are necessary. I chose this particular reading because it is from this reading that I got the title of this book.

I will be using the letter S for the woman being read, and the letter H for myself.

H- She is showing me horses and horse racing.

S- Hera As you can see from her picture she is at Ascot. Thank You.

H- oh I have no idea what that is I'm American lol she showed me horse racing.

H- I can't tell that from the pic.

S- Royal Ascot is a world famous racecourse. She went for ladies day in June this year. Thank you.

H- Oh okay. She was telling me how special it was for her.

Here when I say she is telling me this I am putting the emotion into words.

H- Does someone have a cameo of hers? She is showing me a Cameo which could mean she had one or collected antique jewelry.

Here and with the horses, I say she is showing me these things meaning I am getting a mental picture.

H- Now I am just seeing antiques.

S- Hera, my husband thinks she had one. Not sure who would have it now though. Maybe she could tell you this as she was a very spiritual person. So I would expect her to come through strongly. Thank you.

H- They come through when they are ready and I can only give you what they give me.

I feel this is a good example of letting go of what you want or expect to hear, and just listen to the message that is coming through for you.

S- Her brother collected antiques.

H- I was just getting the horse connection really strong, the cameo and antiques, and a family connection to an English Lord.

H- It might be too soon for a reading I feel like you want to hear a specific detail I might not pick up.

H- Has her husband passed?

H- She says an older male greeted her when she crossed over.

In this instance, I got a visual image of this, and put it into words.

S- The English Lord is from my side of the family.

H- That came through really strong.

S- That could have been her brother or dad. She was very close to both.

S- My family have a habit of being heard lol. X

H- I feel like she saw him in her room shortly before she passed. That was because he was waiting to guide her. I feel like it is an older gentleman so her father most likely.

S- I'm so pleased that her dad came for her. We all thought that it would have been her mother. Thank you.

H- She says tell my son I'm okay I'm happy and safe it was my time to leave. You did everything correctly everything was the way it was meant to be.

S- I know that last she was at the spiritualist church they told her that she had loads of family members around her with their arms open waiting for her. X

H- Does her son have his own business? She is telling me this coming year will be more successful.

H- She passed near the holidays that is really hard I'm sorry for that she says.

H- I feel like there is something else important about that date.

S- Her youngest son doesn't own his own business but he is self-employed and advertises himself. X

H- Thank you for the flowers she says.

S- Not sure about the 6th Dec. If it had been on the 11th Dec. I would of understood. As we mum& me were joking on about going out for my birthday.

H- She says she can re-create the most beautiful garden over here on the other side with the most beautiful flowers.

S- We lived 163 miles away from mum. So when we visited her we took flowers.

S- Mum always had a beautiful garden. Thank you.

H- Ok I kept getting another important date in Dec.

H- She likes to talk right she says it's different from this side lol.

H- She is being very direct with me I am seeing these things so easily.

S- That's how she was. Very direct. She loved to talk. X

H- She keeps going she is a very loving soul.

H- Did she have a problem with her right side?

H- And or her chest?

S- She was beautiful inside and out. We loved her so much. It's hard her not being here.

H- I keep getting a pain in my neck.

S- Yes she did.

H- She loves her family very much she says she will be watching over everyone until we meet again..she says.

H- Oh she wants it to be known she is free of that now. I feel her pulling back now. I hope this reading can bring comfort for you and your family. I'm sorry for your loss.

S-" Until we meet again..she says." She said this in a goodbye letter she left me. Thank you so much. You are an angel sharing such a beautiful gift. Thank you, thank you, thank you for this. Xxxxxx

H- You are very welcome. She did the work I'm just the messenger lol! It was an honor to connect with her. She will connect with your family again via another medium.

S- Bless you for sharing your time with both mum & myself. She was and still is a very special person to me. To me she was more like a birth mother then a mother in-law. I love her deeply. I'm sure it won't be long before she connects again. She did promise to come back & tell me what it is like on the other side. Thank you again..love light & blessings to you & your family. Xxxx

Throughout this reading you can see how spirit used my clairvoyant ability more than any other. Except for the moment when I was feeling her physical problems.

Every reading is different and some readings are more accurate than others. Spirit always come through with the correct information. It is up to me to interpret the message correctly. It is a constant learning experience.

Before you make the decision to visit a medium for a reading you should take your time and be picky about which medium you choose. The first thing you should look for is certification. Certification shows that the medium's skills have been put to the test and are accurate enough to be considered a true professional medium. Word of mouth is also a reliable method in finding a medium that is right for you. If you feel comfortable you can ask family or friends if they have ever had a reading and if they have who they recommend. It is important not to visit a medium to soon after someone has passed. It is important to experience each stage of the grieving process first. Although a reading brings healing when a loss has occurred, it should never be used as a quick fix for our grieve. Everyone grieves differently and in their own time. I recommend waiting at least a year before seeing a medium. When you are ready, it is a good idea to remind yourself of every possible soul that has passed that was close to you. You never know who might pop in and its always a good idea to be prepared for absolutely anyone who might send a message. You also might not hear from the soul you want to the most so be open to any and all of the information that is coming through. Most mediums record their sessions with clients but you might want to bring a notebook to jot down any information you your self are not sure about, and possibly another family member could validate. Also it never hurts to bring a photo of anyone who has passed and or a piece of jewelry. I myself am very skilled with photo reading and psychometry. And the medium you visit may find these items a useful tool. Other tools that maybe used are cards, and writing (automatic). I use a notebook quite often to try and keep up with information that is coming very fast. Before the client arrives the medium may use sage to clear any negative energy that might be present. Before I begin I smudge, and light a white candle that I usually keep burning throughout the reading. I usually have a small bowl of salt nearby as well. I also meditate and call on my guide and Archangel Michael for protection against negative energies. Negative energies can not harm a reading or bring wrong information but they can block information from coming through. If I feel blocked during a reading it is because there is some kind of negative energy present.

Visiting a medium can be one of the most healing and life changing events a person can experience. Taking your time in finding the right medium for you should be taken very seriously. Doing your research and learning how a medium receives their information from the spirit world, may help to remove any fear or apprehension one might have about visiting a medium for the first time. It is not the dramatic experience you might imagine from a Hollywood movie.

If you do your research, let go of expectations, and keep an open mind your experience with a medium should be a memorable, healing, and positive one.

From time to time I will receive a message from a loved one who has passed. The messages I get for myself come through in the same way as they do for others. I receive these messages during automatic writing sessions, dreams, and sometimes out of the blue when I am relaxing. I have to wait for the messages to come to me. The following are two messages that came to me one while I was sitting relaxing, the other in dream. I wrote them down immediately after I got them. They came to me from my paternal grandfather who passed away when I was a year old. I feel these messages are good examples of how to recognize when a loved one who has crossed over is near.

I'm sharing these messages as they appeared as notes on my face book page.

The first note. This was the message I received while just relaxing one afternoon.

Validation

The smell of cigar smoke. Then witnessing a scene from a Boston street circa 1930. Stopping on my way home from a local store, taking off my hat and wiping my brow, feeling the wind blow across my face looking over to admire a maroon colored Model T.

My validation, researching Model T colors of that era and confirming that they did in fact have this coloration. I never knew this until this visitation. I always thought they were gray or black in color. Validation can come in many ways. I almost ignored this piece of information but something just wouldn't let me let it go. A reminder to me to pay close attention to every detail and remember spirit will show you "proof" or validation in the most unexpected ways at times. I am so grateful I can validate my visits with spirit on my own. It is such a comforting feeling to know our loved ones still care, and really want us to know.

The second note, the message I received in a dream.

Saturday Visit

Had an interesting visit while I was napping this afternoon. I was walking on Cole's Hill in my home town of Plymouth Massachusetts. I noticed the dream was black and white. As I was approaching a bench, I saw a man dressed in a 30's style suit and nice looking Fedora. I stopped and thought to myself is that you? He chuckled at my surprise to see him and said yes it's me. It was my paternal grandfather. He looked so handsome, young and happy. He looked as if he didn't have a care and a weight had been lifted from him. He showed me what the spot looked like when he would visit here. And said it was his favorite spot to go and sit and reflect on life. He told me when I come here to look for a sign as proof of our visit.

I can't say that I need proof but I will be looking! I love visits like this. Dreams of passed loved ones always bring happy loving feelings and the feeling of having a deeper connection. I was surprised to have a visit from him in the dream state. I never had the need to due to the fact I have always felt his presence in my life. He passed when I was a baby and I never had the chance to get to know him. I'm not sure why he is there for me but he is. I stopped wondering why and just opened myself to anything he needed to share.

This visit happened shortly before my trip back up north. I am sure he was letting me know he would be there with me in Spirit. One of the signs that was validated the day we visited was the black and white scenery of the dream. It was a dreary, foggy, over cast drizzly day when I went to the spot. As black and white as this reality can get. The weather that day was a sign as well. It was this kind of dreary day the day my Grandmother, his wife passed, which is a tell tale sign of his visit. You will understand why in the next chapter.

Chapter Nine

How To Raise A Psychic Child

I felt this chapter was important to write because I feel those who do not experience the spiritual world the way a medium does, do not realize how big a part of a person's life being psychic and sensing spirit really is. For most it's a far away concept that is truly hard to grasp. For myself it is the biggest part of who I am, and feeling forced to suppress who I was as a young child, caused an already shy and introverted little girl to become an anxiety ridden adult. I am going to discuss how the way I was raised was not the proper environment for someone with my abilities to flourish, and add some advice that would of helped if my parents had the information available to them. Children born with spiritual gifts in this day and age have the advantage of information being easier to access then when I was young. Now there really is no excuse for a parent to turn a blind eye to what is happening with their psychic kids.

This advice comes solely from my own experiences growing up. And is meant to help explain and guide parents in the proper direction.

One instance that comes to my mind and I often think back on is the day father's Mother passed. The day my grandmother passed is a day I will never forget. She was one of the few adults in my life that I felt actual love from. She had an interesting sense of humor and I always felt loved and welcome in her home. The day she passed I was outside playing in the backyard. It was a rainy, foggy, damp, and overcast day. I was jumping over pieces of wood I had found lying around in the backyard. Kind of an obstacle course I made for myself when I was bored. I was jumping around in between light rain drops when suddenly a sense of deep loss came over me. I instantly thought of my grandmother at that same moment. I went inside and as I walked into the kitchen I saw my father hanging up the phone. I asked him what was wrong and he proceeded to give me the sad news that my grandmother had passed away. I looked at him and said I know. He looked at me angrily and said not to ever say things like that again, an walked off. There I was left all alone with my grief and feeling guilty that I knew my grandmother had not only crossed over, but she was okay, happy, and safe and I was never able to tell her son that.

An incident that comes to mind that for me shows my father knew there was something going on with me psychically, happened when I was in junior high school. One evening I was sitting alone at the kitchen table doing my homework when my father sat himself down and announced he was going to try an experiment with me. At the time I was happy to have any sort of what appeared to be positive attention from him. I listened closely as he explained what he had planned. He was going to write something on a piece of paper and put it into a sealed envelope. He instructed me to concentrate on what was in that envelope, at a specific time during the school day, as if I had nothing else I should be concentrating on. And when I came home from school to tell him what I thought he had written. All of this was of course as he put it to see if I could read his mind. Looking back I wonder why he was so nervous about me being able to read his thoughts and I have to giggle. Well I followed his instructions, hoping in the back of my mind I could finally prove my self right and he would actually listen to me. So that afternoon when I came home from school I told him what I thought I saw inside the envelope. He proceeded to look at me blankly and refused to tell me what was in the envelope and if I was right or not. And refused to speak of it again. Looking back I now know I was nothing more than his guinea pig that day. As if his ridiculous experiment was scientifically valid. I have to assume I was correct that day. As far as he was concerned it was more proof for him personally that I really was the evil hell bound entity he treated me as. He was looking to justify the way he treated me and the things he would say. And here I was hoping to finally show of my psychic skills and gain approval.

Looking back from an adult perspective knowing how extreme his religious beliefs really are I think he was afraid of my gift. His religious beliefs had no room for who I was or what I was capable of. I don't think my telekinetic ability helped calm his fears. It does not happen very often, but when it does its an amazing event to witness. At times when I become angry lights will flicker and sometimes light bulbs burst. I have broken ceramic bowls and moved soda cans. One particular night I recall we had just finished having some ice cream. I placed my bowl down beside me on the end table next to the couch I was sitting on. My father walked into the room and said something nasty to me. I became angry and boom the bowl burst into four pieces. I can understand how someone with no understanding of how these events happen would be frightened by seeing something like this happen.

It is because of this I feel so strongly about explaining how psychic events happen and why we really do not need to fear anything paranormal. No parent should feel they need to fear their child, or be under the believe their child is evil. In this regard I feel my father was actually a victim of his beliefs so completely taken over by what he had drilled into his brain that he would tell his child they were condemned to an eternity in hell simply because of who they are.

If you find yourself raising a child with a psychic gift my first word of advice would be to educate yourself as much as possible. Get as many books on the subject as you can. And familiarize yourself with how a psychic perceives their world. If you feel comfortable asking family about experiences they may have had I encourage this. It would be of great comfort for your child to talk openly about his or her experiences with someone else who has also experienced the paranormal. If your child comes to you with information you know they couldn't of known without using their sixth sense, it is important to validate that for them.

When I was a child I was afraid of the dark and to go to sleep at night. I was seeing spirits and feeling the spiritual energy around me in the room. This still happens with me as an adult and I can't fall asleep at night without some sort of light on or the television on. The television distracts me from the spiritual energy and I can effectively ignore it and get to sleep. Also falling asleep to the radio is a good trick as well. When a psychic child wakes from a vivid nightmare, watching television for a bit before going back to sleep works wonders. It takes the mind out of that very scary place and gives us something else to focus on.

Also encourage your child to discuss anything that frightens them and reassure them there are no demons, and nothing can physically hurt them. Teach them to stand up to anything scary by telling them to command them to leave, and surround themselves with white light and Angels. This is a tool they will need for the rest of their lives. They need to know they have the power to get rid of the negative energies on their own.

Also your psychic child needs to know that the information is coming to them. For example your child has a prophetic dream about a tragic event. They need to know they did not cause the event. They knew it was going to happen because they have a special gift. Encourage your child to write down what they dream and what they feel may happen during the day. This will help them identify their intuitive thoughts. Drawing, painting, writing, even working with their hands are all excellent ways for your child to express what is going on with them psychically.

I feel it is important for parents to wait for your children to come to them with their insights. Don't put them on the spot or grill them for information. More often than not we have to wait for the information to come to us, especially when we are children still learning our skills. Also remind them they don't have to share any information with anyone unless they are comfortable with doing so. Not everyone needs to know of their gift especially in childhood when not everyone is going to be welcoming of a child with a gift. We all know childhood and fitting in is hard enough without tacking on psychic gifts.

Another important aspect even though your child may be incredibly psychic, they may not be meant to have a career as a psychic in the future. Expose them to different choices as they grow and trust they will pick the career they were born for.

Understanding, listening, and not putting your psychic child on the spot, are important rules to live by.

Chapter 10

The Future Of Mediumship

Modern day mediumship began with the start of the spiritualist religion. The start of the spiritualist religion began with the Fox family in March of 1848. In 1848, John Fox and his family moved from Canada into a home located in Hydesville, New York. Within a few days of moving in John's wife and two young daughters started to hear un -explainable noises at night that would wake them from their sleep. Mr. Fox would search the home trying to locate the source of the noise but never found anything. He thought they were simply normal random noises. His wife and daughters on the other hand became convinced they were living with a ghost. Mr. Fox continued to search for the source of the noises in order to show the rest of the family there was no ghost among them. One night Mr. Fox was checking for evidence that it was simply the noises of an unfamiliar house everyone was hearing. He was knocking on door frames and window sills. As he was knocking, his daughter Kate noticed that the ghost was knocking back. When her father knocked, the same number of knocks would come back in reply. Kate then began to speak to the unseen presence calling it out loud by a nickname her and her sister had given it "Mr. Splitfoot." She asked the ghost to answer her by knocking in response to her knocks. The ghost then began to answer Kate with the same number of knocks she sent out. When the rest of the family noticed, Mrs. Fox took the opportunity to try and communicate with the entity as well. She began asking questions that could be answered numerically. She asked the ages of her children including the age of the child who had recently passed away. The entity responded correctly each time. A neighbor who had heard about what was happening in the home, and was also a former tenant, William Dueslur, also wanted to try a communication with the unseen presence. He created an alphabet using a series of knocks. He used a number of knocks for yes and a number for no. Using his method he was able to figure out who the entity was. In front of a group of witnesses he was able to determine that the entity was the spirit of a peddler who had been murdered and robbed years before. One of the witnesses was the former maid of the previous owners the Bell family. The maid, Lucretia Pulver, came forward to say that she had found dirt that looked as if it had been disturbed in the cellar. John Fox and William Deusler went to the cellar and began to dig where the maid had described. As they dug they found a piece of bone with hair still attached to it. They also came across some pieces of tattered clothing. The two men brought the piece of bone to a local doctor who confirmed it was from a human skull. They became convinced the spirit in the house was in fact that of the peddler. Shortly after the story took a dramatic turn. The two daughters claimed to have mediumistic powers. The news began to spread quickly. By November 1849 the two sisters were giving public performances of their new skills and the modern spiritualist movement was born. The mania to communicate with the dead swept the country and the Fox sisters became famous.

Although mediumship as we know it today began with the spiritualist movement, not every medium are of the spiritualist faith. Mediums today are Catholic, Gnostic, and some belong to the neo-pagan groups such as Wicca and Witchcraft. Most mediums who seek out classes and or workshops are trained in a similar fashion. The only exception being those who use divination tools such as cards, scrying mirrors, or similar tools. Although mediums go through similar training methods, each medium brings their own personality and style to spirit communication.

The mediums in the public eye today have brought their gifts to the masses through television, radio, books, and the internet. Large group readings are another popular way today's mediums share their gifts with the public.

Spirit has a plan. It is not by accident that people are moving away from traditional religions as mediumship has been working itself into the mainstream. The more people see mediums on television, and read their books, the more the public has been able to drop the fear and mysticism associated with psychic phenomenon. The public is able to see that mediums are normal everyday people, born with the exceptional gift of being able to connect with the world of spirit.

I feel one of the major reasons people are seeking an alternative to traditional religion is that people are searching for evidence they can validate that there is in fact life after death. A message brought by a medium from a loved one who has crossed, is the ultimate validation that life goes on after this one ends. Receiving a message from the other side also gives a level of healing that traditional religions may not be able to provide. A medium connecting with a loved one and sending a message from the other side shows us all that not only do our souls live on after death, but our loved ones are safe, loved, at peace, and more importantly still apart of our daily lives.

Mediumship has had a slow evolution emerging into the mainstream. More and more people are becoming open to the idea, and accepting that our loved ones can in fact communicate with us from beyond the grave.

The first mediums that were brave enough to through themselves in front of the public and bring spirit communication out from the shadows, have made it an easier road for those like myself to do the same. Those like myself will in turn make it easier for the next generation and so on.

Mediumship today will open up a new world and new understanding of what life on this planet truly means, show people the difference between being a religious person and a spiritual one, and give those who seek a new way to discover the answers they are looking for.